D1115005

EDITH
STEIN

jean de fabregues

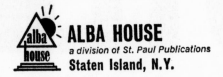

ALBA HOUSE
a division of St. Paul Publications
Staten Island, N.Y.

EDITH
STEIN

Translated from the French by Donald M. Antoine, St. Thomas Seminary, Kenmore, Washington

Original title: La Conversion d' Edith Stein, published by Wesmael-Charlier, Paris

The publisher wishes to express thanks to the Carmelites of the Convent Maria vom Frieden, 5 Koln, Vor den Siebenburgen, Germany, for help in procuring the cover photograph of Edith Stein

Nihil Obstat: John A. Goodwine, J.C.D., Censor Librorum

Imprimatur: Terence J. Cooke, V.G.

New York, N.Y.
June 9, 1965

The nihil obstat and imprimatur are offical declarations that a book or pamphlet is free of doctrinal or moral error. No implication is contained therein that those who have granted the nihil obstat and imprimatur agree with the contents, opinions or statements expressed.

Library of Congress Catalog Card Number: 65-25849

Designed, printed and bound in the U.S.A. by the Pauline Fathers and Brothers.

Alba House is staffed by the Pauline Fathers and Brothers of the Society of St. Paul, Staten Island, N.Y. All the operations going into the making of this book, from editing to binding, were carried out by the Fathers and Brothers as part of their publishing apostolate. The Society was founded in 1914, to spread Christ's message by means of the press, radio, motion pictures and television.

EDITH STEIN

CONTENTS

EDITH STEIN

PREFACE

I have chosen to write the biography of this martyred German Jewish woman for three reasons, all of which pierce right to the heart of the drama of our times in its totality. They show how this is a human and a spiritual drama. And, in the course of it, these three reasons combine to form the center of Edith Stein's personal drama.

Edith Stein was every inch a philosopher—a type of the modern "intellectual". She was called upon to sacrifice herself, and she consented wholeheartedly. But she was asked to give up much more than her life, for such a sacrifice would have been over within just a few minutes. Edith agreed to sacrifice her intellectual activity—her special gift—because God asked it of her through the Rule of her convent which was the voice of the Church, and therefore the will of God.

Edith Stein was an "existentialist" philosopher.

She took part in the first beginnings of this movement which is highly respected today, though it is
somewhat debased. Working in the very heart of
"existentialism", she came to examine its depth and
gauge its truth values.

This existentialist philosopher sought no mitiga-
ted form of the Church's spiritual life; she sought no
kind of slanted Catholic thought, or any thought
which made compromises with the so-called "modern
ideas". She lived the perfect spiritual life of prayer
and contemplation in the convent. She studied St.
Thomas Aquinas, the traditional philosopher of the
Church, and felt that he expressed her own conclusions on God and the world better than anyone
else. She was certain that the Church best answered
the "modern" questions.

Through her seemingly plotted-out vocation,
Edith Stein answered the most puzzling questions of
our times. During her religious life, Edith declared
that the most stringent philosophy of the Church
had solved her particular philosophical difficulties.
She, as an existentialist, took up the philosophy of
Being and found the key to Existence in it. She
discovered and offered us the united and inseparable
aspects of the All-Powerful and All-Loving one:
Prayer, Truth and total Being. Armed with the
Faith and the most rigorous of thought, she grap-
pled with the material world in all its dimensions

and answered its problems through them. From the beginning to the end, this daughter of the Synagogue kept her "stiff-neck", making absolutely no compromises with God, herself or the age in which she lived.

She mapped out the long journey from Absolute Exigency to the boundless Response, as did some other women such as Rhaïssa Maritain and Simone Weil, to mention two whom I knew and who have since died. How can Catholics today not be inspired by such examples as theirs?

Edith Stein taught us one final lesson: her first glimpse into the Catholic Faith at the Adolph Reinach home was of two people converted during the First World War. Thus, she teaches us that the Catholic Church continues in the heart of the "modern world" in which we believe that everything is, at each instant, renewed. Edith, we are always heirs, bringing to the Church the message of the Synagogue, the philosophical message of the most "modern" of philosophical movements. We are mindful of this fact from the very outset.

EDITH STEIN

1   A STRICT JEWISH FAMILY AND A GIRL
EAGER FOR PRECISION

October 12, 1891, on the Jewish feast of the Expiation, called the Atonement,[1] a girl was born in
Breslau (Silesia) into a Jewish family of strict observance and deep faith. Her father, Siegfried Stein,
had been in the timber business there for about a
year; her mother's name, surprisingly enough, was
French—Augusta Courant. Edith was barely two
years old when Siegfried Stein died, leaving his wife
with seven children to care for by running his timber concern. Edith was the youngest of these children. People said that if this business had not already been prosperous when she inherited it from
her husband, Frau Stein would soon have made it
so. She could buy up whole forests, knew how to
judge standing timber, and made business trips
across Silesia to the Balkans. She still ran the house-

1 Also called the Day of Reconciliation.

hold at the age of eighty-eight. Both parents came from large families: the Steins had twenty-two children (from three mothers), and the Courants had fourteen children from one mother. While running her business, Augusta Courant would still take time off to bake the family's bread, and at first it was difficult going for her. But not for long. Frau Stein bought a fine stone house and the children were able to continue their various educations uninterrupted. The eldest, Elsa, taught for a time and then married. One of the boys, Paul, entered into baking, while a second, Arno, helped his mother run the timber business. A second daughter, Erika, married and after a time left her husband to return home to live with her mother. Rosa lived at home, and another daughter, Erna, became a doctor.

In Germany, particularly in Silesia, the years from 1890 to 1900 were years for the massive development of industry and commerce. The era of Bismark bore fruit. The Jewish world of Germany might easily have become swallowed up and forgotten in the great commercial expansion, and in fact many Jews did actually lose their faith or play down the role of the religious side of their lives. But the Steins did no such thing and remained staunchly loyal to the Synagogue. The atmosphere of the Stein household was both one of work and strict religious observance: prayer and worship. They prayed in Hebrew

before and after meals, and they often prayed such
prayers as the incomparable Prayer of Solomon
which expressed the hope "that all the people of
the earth might come to know that the Eternal is
God and that there is no other".

They fasted when it was proper for them to do
so, and they followed the other obligations of the
Synagogue. They washed their dishes in several
washes as prescribed. But above all, God was present
to them. "My mother believed in God with all her
heart," Edith's sister, Erna Biberstein, wrote, "and
she had complete confidence in Him." Much later,
when Edith, then a Catholic, had gone with her
mother to the Synagogue in order to ease the pain of
her conversion, the Rabbi read the traditional text:
"Hear O Israel, your God is One", Frau Stein repeated
it back to Edith, alluding to the dogma of the Holy
Trinity. When Edith read "right conduct in her
mother's heart", as she herself wrote, "to know how
to live", it was this faith and this love of God she
saw there with all its interior strength and that
intensity which makes up the Jewish temperament.
And from that time on Edith knew that if there were
a God, He had to be loved and served with this
determination and honesty.

The Day of Atonement, Edith's birthday, was the
last of the ten days the Jewish calendar calls the
"Bitter Days" or the "Austere Days". It is the height

of the Jewish spiritual year. On that day, and that
day alone, the Jew kneels down and "There he does
what he refused to do before the king of the Persians.
He does what no power on earth could move him to
do, what he does at no time of the year before anyone, not even God. And if he kneels, it is not to
confess a fault or beg forgiveness of sins, though this
is the purpose of the feast, rather, he kneels because
he recognizes the immediate nearness of God. . . .
The Day of Atonement, the crowning point of the
ten days of redemption, is justly called the Sabbath
of Sabbaths. The assembly quickens to the awareness of the divine presence when it calls to mind
the Temple of former days, particularly that moment
when the High Priest, on this singular occasion of
the year, pronounced the ineffable name of God,
unspoken at any other time except through cir-
cumlocution."[2]

Born on the Day of Atonement, the child Edith
was destined to ascend to "the immediate nearness
of God" and to *call* Him by His own name, not just
once, but daily and at every moment of her life. She
would make the presence and the call of God her
own through His name. There is a direct bond and
an unswerving union from the One God—but One
in Three—to the little Jewess of Breslau who was

2 Franz Rosenzweig, *L'anné Juive.*

destined to become one of the foremost philosophers of the twentieth century, and above all, the bride of our Lord.

Those who knew Edith before her conversion have depicted her as "cold and distant". One schoolgirl friend described her "always unnoticed among us, in spite of her reputation for extreme intelligence ... she seemed somewhat old-fashioned to us ... always sitting up front in the auditorium, a mere slip of a girl—tiny, almost insignificant, and absorbed in the intensity of her thoughts. Her hair was dull and sleek and she wore it coiffed in headbands and fastened together at the neck in a heavy bun. She had an almost sickly palor, and her large black eyes, with their intense gaze, became stern—almost distant—as if fighting off all distractions. But as soon as one got to know her personally, an indescribable kindliness lit up her eyes, a delightful smile animated her face, and these little traits hinted of the candor and timidity of childhood. One cannot say she was either beautiful or even pretty, nor that she possessed that womanly charm which is so attractive .... But there was something incomparable in her face, from the high intellectual forehead to the marvelously expressive childlike traits—a refreshing glow—difficult not to admire."[3]

3 Sister Aldegonde Jaegerschmidt, OSB. Radio broadcast message on the tenth anniversary of Edith Stein's death (Stuttgart,

I never knew Edith Stein. But as I read these lines I cannot help but think back on two other women, Rhaïssa Maritain and Simone Weil, whom I knew and whose spiritual development was so parallel to Edith's. There is that same lessening of strong physical appearances in face of the intellectual and spiritual might, even the profound intensity of gaze which expresses the soul with, perhaps, some of Simone Weil's impetuous will for expression that Edith did not at first have. Simone Weil kept her eyes open first on the world and then later on souls, while Edith lifted hers right up to God. Edith's was a contemplative vocation, and this interior call seems evident from childhood. She found strength in silence and an interior life which would culminate in communication with God. The days Edith were to spend in prayer and contemplation before the Blessed Sacrament are signs of this. The interior life governed everything about her and showed up beautifully in her relations with people whom she treated with the fullness of charity. Simone Weil progressed from humanity to God; Edith encountered mankind through God.

Edith possessed the spirit of empathy. Sister Aldegonde Jaegerschmidt noted Edith's early "knack

1952), cf. Sister Teresia de Spiritu Sancto, trans. Hastings and Nicholl, Sheed and Ward (London, 1952).

for teaching" when she helped out students, lost in the vocabulary of Husserl, by giving them introductory notions by which they could find themselves: "She formed us with endless patience, an attentive and quiet generosity. Always friendly, without the least irony of criticism, she welcomed our awkward questions with a calmness, and even temper and dedication, so much so that we would scarcely give her a minute's peace! ... Untiringly, she nudged us a little further along the foreboding path to intellectual knowledge. The zeal which consumed her won our hearts...."[4]

One person who knew Edith before her conversion shows her at that time viewing creatures with a "detached, penetrating expression, the very mien of a judge". She "gave us the impression of a wholly integrated personality in full control of itself".

Thoughts of despair and confusion had no part in Edith Stein's conversion, neither did the discontentment peculiar to some people searching "elsewhere" for the equilibrium they could not find *here*. Hers was an intellectual conviction and a judgment of the world, its existence and its meaning. One might say Edith's conversion was not a *psychological* conversion, a conversion based on personal needs, but

[4] Sister Aldegonde Jaegerschmidt, OSB.

rather that it was an *intellectual* and *spiritual* conversion, the two being united and constantly parallel.
The judgment of her mind and the desire of her soul
looked for God as the one necessity for existence—
not so much her own existence among mankind, but
the existence of all creation, the existence of the
whole world acknowledging its source and meaning.
The physical portrait of Edith has already told us
what her whole life would constantly stress.

As a child, Edith had a yearning for the absolute
which was later to govern her thought. This desire
for the absolute first showed up in a childhood dis-
appointment. Brought up with her brothers and
sisters of all ages, she not only joined in with their
games, but wished to understand them: they en-
hanced her mental precocity, and, when at the age
of four they sent her to a nursery-school because she
wanted to go to school "like the other children", she
returned home defeated and inconsolably unhappy
for being debased by the infantile atmosphere of the
school.

Her elder brother, carrying her in his arms, taught
her the names of the German poets and the titles
of their works. When they played at home the game
called *Dichter-quartett,*[5] the child of four years

5 Difficult to translate. Possibly something like "the troop of
poets" or "the poet corner".

amazed the family guests because she knew the names of the authors and could assign to each their own works. At this age, her companions thought her "deep, reserved, quiet" but "always obliging and understanding". And, when she did not get the very highest marks at school, she said at home, "Mother, forgive me for not achieving the best grades. Hilda got them, and it is better because she doesn't have any mother." The absolute of understanding could conceive of giving way only to the absolute of charity.

Edith began school on her sixth birthday, October 12, in the middle of the school year which began in Germany at Easter.[6] In spite of this disadvantage, by Christmas she was one of the very best in the class.

In 1906, when she was fifteen, Edith left school. We might ask why. She received the highest marks, but never was given the first place which all her companions insisted she deserved. Her biographers think she was prejudiced against on account of the headmaster's anti-Semitism. At any rate, she went to live with her married sister Elsa, now the mother of three children, to help with the housekeeping, and she was quick to learn that that kind of life was

6 cf. Hilda C. Graef, *The Scholar and the Cross,* Newman Press (1955).

not for her. Edith returned home to her mother and
made up for lost time by special tutoring, so that
she passed the *Studienanstalt* in 1908, and in 1911
the final comprehensive examinations which led to
higher studies.[7]

Frau Stein's remarkable personality dominated
Edith's life at home. Edith wrote, "At home it was
not a matter of education exactly. As children we
read right conduct in our mother's example as if in
a mirror of the virtues. Mother taught us the horror
of sin. And when she said 'That is a sin', she conveyed
the idea of all that is hateful and ugly, and we lived
in dread of it."[8]

Edith's studies gave her a well-rounded education.
She was fluent in French, English, Spanish, Latin,
Greek, and of course Hebrew. At twenty years of
age she enrolled into the University of Breslau, in
her native land, to take courses in history and philo-
logy and experimental psychology.

Quite early in life Edith lost her Jewish religion
because she denied the existence of God. Yet, she
continued to accompany her mother to the Synagogue
to spare her the pain of her daughter's disbelief.

In Breslau she read Husserl's *Logical Investigations* which quickened her mind to that train of

---

7 cf. Sister Teresia de Spiritu Sancto, ODC, *Edith Stein.*
8 Sister Teresia de Spiritu Santo, ODC, *Edith Stein.*

thought which would become her own. Because Husserl taught at Göttingen, she went there to continue her higher education, and her mother's cousin, Richard Courant, himself a professor of mathematics at the university, welcomed her.

"I was twenty-one years old," wrote Edith, "and I was full of eager anticipation. Psychology had deceived me. I had come to the conclusion that this science was still in its infancy and lacked an objective foundation. But the little I knew of phenomenology delighted me, particularly the objective method of investigation."

In her opinion, phenomenology was Husserl. And he taught at Göttingen. Her family raised no objections to her studying there, so she embarked upon the intellectual journey which would influence her until she had come to realize the first and complete reality which is God.

Her classmates made up a song about Edith when she left Breslau, as was the tradition, and they gave it the title "The Objective Expert". Objectivity was just coming into the fore in the philosophical world. Kantian and post-Kantian idealism had long dominated both the entire German intellectual world and most of the French. At the same time, experimental psychology, a discipline which attracted Edith's attention, was totally limited to observation of exterior human acts. The human person seemed torn between the distant world of abstract ideas and a reality limited only to what the senses could directly perceive. How could one such as Edith, driven by that impassioned search for truth, put up with a dichotomy of being which could never lead to any religious faith?

EDITH STEIN

2 THE PHILOSOPHY OF BEING LEADS
EDITH STEIN TO THE FAITH

Love and intellectual conviction were at the root
of Edith Stein's conversion. If this seems paradoxical,
let us show how and why the conversion of the
little Jewess of Breslau is one of the most significant
in modern drama and in Catholicism.

Her conversion came about through love and
not emotionalism. Edith Stein suffered a great deal,
be assured of that. She endured much all her life,
and early in life, as for example, when though certainly the brightest pupil in school, the headmaster
refused to acknowledge her superiority because of
his anti-Semitism. And when she returned home
from school, instead of brooding and crying over
this injustice, she tried to find reasons to justify it
to her mother so that she could rejoice in her school-
mate's success. She suffered intensely when she attended the Synagogue with her mother after she had
lost her faith. Edith suffered when she sensed her

mother's grief over her daughter's "infidelity". She
endured great pain in the heartache she caused her
mother with her conversion to Catholicism, departure
from home and her entry into the religious life. She
suffered still more during the Nazi persecutions.

Edith never expressed the grief welling up from
within her soul. Her love was totally foreign to any
emotionalism in the bad sense, because hers was a
contemplative love. How else can one explain Edith's
ecstacy before her God in the Eucharist, her complete absorption in His infinite presence? We do not
find it difficult depicting this girl, who rarely showed
her feelings, wholly *absorbed* in the contemplation
of Him Who Is. Nothing but love could sustain such
a silent dialogue.

The sharpened edge of her intellect came to
realize its cause and final end—this was the food of
her dialogue with God. Her intellect saw the infinite
necessity of an infinite being who is infinite Love.
She contemplated Him and listened to Him speak
to her mind the language of Absolute Presence and
Absolute Necessity in which she saw her cause.

This tiny woman's response to the infinite showed
her the Being without whom she would be nothing.

* * *

At Göttingen, the philosopher Edmund Husserl,
one of the first teachers of phenomenology and exis-

tentialism, opened her mind to the revelation of being.

Almost by sheer chance Edith began to read Husserl's *Logical Investigations,* and this same chance brought her and Erna to their cousin's home in Göttingen.

This 'bit of chance' was to open whole new horizons to her and quell one of her deepest longings: "Psychology had deceived me. I had come to the conclusion that this science was still in its infancy and lacked an objective foundation. But the little I knew of phenomenology delighted me, particularly the objective method of investigation." In a world of idealism and relativism that questioned the validity of the mind, she suddenly caught the glimmering of a light, and something dared whisper the words *reality* and *truth* to her. Edith accepted and turned wholeheartedly to this light.

After Husserl went to the Sorbonne in 1929 to deliver several conferences there, Benjamin Fondane described him in this way: "He is neither a miracle-worker nor a preacher. Beneath the guise of a humble provincial is a man who radiates the virtues of order and decency. You could call it shyness if there hadn't been something sensual and provocative in his be-spectacled looks. He pretends to be but a man of science, mindful only of *describing* the laws and

basic structures of consciousness, hesitant to delve
into reality or get in its way, trying to be rigorous
by readily accepting everything, exaggerating nothing if possible, but overlooking nothing . . . . His mod-
esty comes from the fact that he serves us absolute
truth and not his own truth."[1]

"This humble provincial" was to set Edith in the
right direction. Because he only wanted to "describe
reality", he "ignored nothing and believed not in
his truth, but in an *absolute truth* . . . ."

At Göttingen he taught Edith that "truth is an
absolute", that it "is not the creation of one who
perceives it."[2] He taught that one must discover
the primary truths in themselves upon which the
entire structure of universal knowledge rests.[3] When
he asked how he could seriously question himself
about how to escape from the island of his consciousness, since it was clearly evident that his consciousness could attain to objective meaning, he ran up
against what had obstructed every philosophy of
reality and existence from the time of Descartes, and
which gave rise to innumerable idealisms and rela-
tivisms which were but various disguises of skepticism.[4] He resolved that he could get away from the

1 B. Fondane, *La Conscience Malheureuse.*
2 Edmond Husserl, *Logical Investigations.*
3 Edmond Husserl, *Cartesian Meditations.*
4 Ibid.

island of his consciousness, but said it would be folly to try to define a state of consciousness because the very structure of life remains when the "phenomena" pass away, and this "structure" evades all one's doubt and relativism. There is a "universal foundation for the experience of the ego".

Edith was attracted to Husserl's desire to investigate things as they are[5] to find out what they have to tell us, as Husserl himself stated and the second great phenomenologist, Heidegger, reiterated.

At Juvisy in 1932, a German Benedictine monk, Dom Feuling, working with the *Société de Philosophie Thomiste,* explained the phenomenological thinkers to the German Catholic world, and in the course of his work outlined Husserl's basic ideas with these words: "His work will be complete only when it leads us to the first origin of all that is created, to the first being in which and through which all other beings ... with their actions and their objects, are originally constituted—to the truly absolute ego who alone constitutes everything and Who is Himself uncreated—to God who lives His life in creating ...."

Edith Stein immediately perceived Husserl's desire to advance beyond all philosophical systems to reach out to the heart of true reality and the founda-

5 We shall not go into its implications or values.

tion of life. She was, of course, unaware that her path led to God "creating everything which is created", as Dom Feuling illustrated. Without realizing it, she desired to discover the *Source* of all reality. In addition, when she helped out at Juvisy in 1932, where Dom Feuling translated Husserl, she spoke of Husserl in this vein: "the phenomenological method is a process of *revelation* which transcends the world as we know it—it is a description of actions and of bodies of actions . . . ." And, mentioning without stressing the fact that she had not followed Husserl's philosophical evolution, Edith Stein noted during her "Days at Juvisy" that what had characterized Husserl's early pupils in the Göttingen period, herself included—was an orientation into the meaning of objective essences which had in due course given the impression of a Scholastic renewal.[6]

Husserl's philosophy is a praise of the concrete, as for example when he spoke of a red object's "redness" as the red object itself and not the abstraction of the genus "redness". He said we perceive an object as it is. No amount of rationalization can make one hold them as non-existent because it is the mind itself which perceives them. Husserl

6 *Compte rendu des Journées de Juvisy*: *"La Phénoménologie", Editions du Cerf.*

wrote that the only truly absolute being was the pure intellect.[7]

At Juvisy, Edith Stein spoke of the "plenitude of essence and being which pervades the subject of the experience in every true experience, and extending beyond the evidence of the consciousness, escapes every possibility of grasping it." It was extremely important for her to realize this because it showed that she saw immediately in Husserl's work the mind's immediate awareness of the existence of the world, which is a grasp so direct upon the reality of the world, that no sophism could undo it. At the same time, we begin to see the direction of her thought: we are aware of the existence of the universe; it *pervades* us and eludes our every attempt to "grasp and express it"; God speaks to us in the reality of the world's existence; He is there, behind all things, He and He alone who Is, and therefore, to be receptive to the voice of the world speaking to one's consciousness is to be receptive to God, to hear Him speaking. Edith had soared to the very brink of contemplation.

Because Husserl had not resolved his intuition[8] to its ultimate conclusion and avoided such a conclusion by putting the question of the actual exis-

7 Edmond Husserl, *Formal and Transcendental Logic.*

8 In philosophy only. He had come quite close to Christ before his death.

tence of the exterior world as perceived by the
mind "into parentheses" he shut himself off from
the only effective way out of idealism and skepticism, as Jacques Maritain has conclusively shown
us.[9] Edith perfected his philosophy by seeing there
is no third alternative between the acceptance and
refusal of the reality of existence, and that if, through
our "consciousness", we come into contact with
something, we must surely admit that something
does in fact exist.

* * *

Edith went to Göttingen to attend Husserl's lec-
tures. Göttingen, a small university town of thirty
thousand inhabitants, is banked all around with
forested hillsides. Romantic castles dominate the
Weser Valley, and thick walls hem in the city. The
Town-Hall is of course Gothic in design, as it ought
to be, and the central square displays the traditional
water fountain. One of the Hanseatic cities, Göttingen is steeped in an ever-present sense of history.
The Grimm brothers as well as Heine and Bismark
studied there. At Göttingen the students made the
most of the life in the streets and taverns in the
cleared woods, while they hid their rooms behind
windows made of stained bottle glass. On the re-

9 Jacques Maritain, *The Degrees of Knowledge.*

gularly scheduled evenings they sang in the taverns and held their customary meetings to which they came decked out in traditional hats and ribbons and carried swords at their side.

Edith Stein came to Göttingen on April 17, 1913, in her twenty-first year, with her friend Rosa Guttmann, a mathematician. They took two rooms at a "boarding house", keeping one set aside for a living and work-room. Edith rarely mixed in with such student festivities as dance nights (ritually scheduled for Wednesdays and Sundays). Instead, she tramped up and down the nearby forests and wandered over the hills of the Hartz Mountains—those "seas of stone" and "haunted rocks" where sorcerers once gathered to dance upon the nights of the Witches' Sabbath. The little Jewess of Breslau sought out the meaning of the world in Nature—she was keenly in harmony with it—as well as in text books.

Husserl was a professor and it was not his place to meet a young, unknown scholar. Such things he left to his assistant, Adolph Reinach, who was still quite a young man. At that time, he was thirty years old and fated to die shortly in World War I. Reinach was a Jew. German philosophy of that time abounded in Jewish philosophers. The Reinachs were an upper-class Jewish family, and in spite of all his advantages, he lived in a kind of strange sadness which nothing seemed to justify. He was married and deeply in love, considerate to all who knew him, beloved of all. We can only account for this sadness in that he had not yet discovered what he searched for so intensely and was soon to find: a genuine hope. He bravely examined the world to discover this hope, and as he said, "One must not be afraid of ultimate realities." But to him it seemed that the night was filled with the gelatinous and gloomy mass of pantheism. This most interesting man had set out on the road ahead of Edith and Providence had led Edith to him.

For quite some time Adolph Reinach lived at the very brink of the Faith. He wrote that Christianity was "the meeting place of all the great classical developments", and admitted to Dietrich von Hildebrand that the Trinity is the only acceptable concept of God.[10] However, Reinach did not truly embrace the Faith until after several months at the front, in 1915. He wrote to his wife, also on the verge of conversion, "The first weeks were frightening, then God's peace came into me, and now all is well." The Reinach Edith Stein met was still a restless, intense man. She wrote, "Never have I been received with such kindness by anyone ... it was as though a whole new world had opened up to me."

10 J. M. Oesterreicher, *Sept philosophes juifs devant le Christ, Editions du Cerf.*

Several days later, Edith met Husserl in person and he struck her the same way, according to Alexandre Koyré—a pupil of his at the time[11]—as one who staggered everyone who listened to him. He had the knack of uprooting them from the mire of skepticism by showing them a glimpse of reality.

From Koyré to Dietrich von Hildebrand, everyone agreed that Husserl soon took note of Edith and began paying her special attention. Frau Husserl was more difficult to win over, but Edith succeeded, though that woman "had the habit of nonplusing her husband's best pupils with her trenchant and ironical remarks."

Edith continued her classes with Max Scheler at Göttingen and apparently received her first glimmer of the light of the Gospels through him. Everything seemed to direct her to the study of human life in its reality—Scheler's philosophy was indeed a cry of one alone in the wilderness. He studied the degrees of sympathy, the meanings of suffering, relationships between beings, the meaning of resentment and heroism, wisdom and holiness. At a time when philosophy was but the history of reason and ideas, reflections on scientific knowledge, or the birth-pangs of sociology, Scheler was a true precursor.

11 Today a professor at the Sorbonne.

Scheler's life, devoted to the study of the tragical human being, itself developed into a tragedy, like Kierkegaard's, his forerunner. He was a Jew through his mother's side of the family. He received Baptism and shortly, caught up in the whirlwind of a passionate love affair, married a divorcee and cut himself off from the Church. The reverberations of his conjugal life forced him to relinquish his professorship at the university, and, at Göttingen, he taught in a small café while he went to Beuron Abbey to try to find that peace of mind which finally came with his re-entry into the Church.[12] Edith, who wrote of herself, "the thirst after truth was my only prayer", listened to Scheler more closely than to Husserl: "He was an extremely fascinating man. He even looked like a genius. I have never experienced the phenomenon of genius in any other person. He was handsome, and his blue eyes seemed to radiate the glow of a higher world. Yet, his life left its etchings on his noble features, and made one think—irresistably—of Oscar Wilde's *A Portrait of Dorian Gray* . . . . He spoke with great emphasis, sometimes dramatically, and always captivated his audience . . . ."

This zealous girl went after Truth with all her might. Usually young girls especially are completely

12 Scheler ultimately left the Church.

carried away by their admiration for their teachers, Edith's whole being cried for such enthusiasm. She decided to write her thesis on the *Einfühlung*—a difficult word to translate; sometimes "empathy" suffices, but we rather think it "intuition by sympathy".

Edith explained her choice: "In his course on Nature and Spirit, Husserl maintained one could only experience an objective external world intersubjectively, that is, by a plurality of knowing individuals who can communicate experiences with one another. Such an exterior world presupposes the experience of other individuals. Husserl, following Theodore Lipps, called this experience *Einfühlung* (empathy), but did not explain what it consisted of. This was a gap worth filling: I wanted to find out what empathy meant."

Edith devoted her work to the study of human relationships and their meaning. Scheler came upon Edith's path at just the right moment. He gave her much more than a philosophical contribution in that he planted an idea in her mind—an idea which constantly grew: "For myself, as for many others, his influence extended far beyond the bounds of philosophy. I do not know in what year Scheler returned to the Catholic Church, but it cannot have been long afterwards, for he was overflowing with Christian ideas and expressed them with all the brilliance of his mind and power of expression. *For me it was the unfolding of a whole new world which until then had remained completely unknown to me, but it still did not lead me to the Faith.* Aside from that, he did open up a vast new realm of phenomena before my eyes, and I could no longer ignore it . . . . The fetters of the rationalism in which I had been brought up without realizing it shook loose and I suddenly found myself encountering the world of faith. People with whom I came into contact every day and whom I admired lived in that world, and I thought that it at least deserved some investigation. I made no systematic examination into this religion, because my mind was still too absorbed with other things. I remained open to the influences of my environment and accepted their influence almost without noticing it."

She was "receptive" to her environment because it satisfied needs of which she was hardly aware. A bond was knotted, a sheaf of wheat gathered together for the harvest. From Husserl she learned that the mind reveals the existence of a profound reality which sustains existence. Scheler taught her that we cannot really experience the reality of the world except in relation to others who illuminate us with a sense of presence because it is a relationship of love, an expression of harmony towards . . . towards what? That profound reality sustaining the universe.

What do you call it? What is this being that is more intensely in existence than all creation, that being which gives creation its being and reveals its existence? Edith took note of life going on around her during these months, as she had always, and Scheler taught her what being aware of others meant. While on a hike up in the mountains, she had to unexpectedly spend the night at a farm. In the morning she awoke to the sound of the household at prayer before beginning the day's work. She found that unknown reality among them, present to them and shared in by them.

During her time at Göttingen, Edith frequently took time off from her studies to trek through the countryside of Protestant Thuringia and the Hartz, taking note of Luther's influence, Weimar and the tombs of Goethe and Schiller, the results of a rationalistic or romantic philosophy thought to be the apex of human wisdom. These things did not impress her because she had advanced far beyond them on her way to truth.

In 1914, the war interrupted her intellectual life, but she patched together what she could when Husserl, newly-appointed to Freiburg, asked her to accompany him as his assistant. She accepted. But He who was patiently calling and waiting for her had a special destiny mapped out for her.

That same summer of 1916, while Edith lived

at Freiburg, Adolph and Anna Reinach decided to
become Protestants. Reinach questioned his motives:
"Might it be that I am not yet ready to join the
Catholic Church?" Anna—later a Catholic—thought
"that once in communion with Christ, He would lead
us where He willed". The following year, in November, Reinach was killed in Flanders and Anna requested Edith to arrange his philosophical papers.
It frightened Edith to think about going to the
Reinach home and finding there, instead of "a happy
young couple", only the somber shadows of deep
mourning. To her surprise, "far from being discon-
solate", it was Anna herself who lent strength to
her late husband's friends "on account of her un-
shakable faith in a living God."

"It was', Edith confided much later, "my first
encounter with the Cross and the divine strength
it inspires in those who carry it. For the first time,
I saw the Church born out of the Passion of Christ
and victorious over death. At that moment my unbelief was utterly crushed, Judaism paled before
my eyes, and the light of Christ poured into my
heart—the light of Christ in the mystery of the
Cross. Because of this light, I desired to take the
habit of the Carmel that I might be called into the
"Order of the Cross"...."

Seven years passed before her Baptism on January
1, 1922. But the two converging paths of philosophi-

cal and human evidence, of philosophical and human necessity, finally met. The existence of the world was a fact which intellectual awareness recognizes and encounters, but the underlying reality, the essential being, is He who gave Anna and Adolph Reinach the grace to be what they were because they were of the Church and in the Church.

Observing the union between Anna and her husband, Edith noted: "At that moment, my unbelief left me", not because of some vague recognition of an unknown spiritual power, but because of the strength of Christ and His Cross which the Church shares in. Therein lay the source of Anna Reinach's peace, and the fount of the peasants' joy in their prayer before setting off to work....

EDITH STEIN

3 THE MEANING OF EXISTENCE: HER ENCOUNTER WITH TERESA OF AVILA AND HER BAPTISM

On August 3, 1916, Edith Stein passed the oral examination of her thesis at the University of Freiburg where Husserl taught under a full professorship, and she received her degree under him *summa cum laude*. Edith joyfully took up his offer to have her as his private assistant. She took Reinach's place, vacant since he went off to war and to which he would never return. Among her many new duties, she had to transcribe all of Husserl's shorthand notes.[1] Edith began this undertaking after her encounter with the converted Anna Reinach and after she had arranged his notes.

There was no apparent change in her: she took her usual long excursions around Freiburg, the Black

[1] Edith found literally tens of thousands of shorthand notes waiting for her. These are now preserved in the *Archives Husserl* at Louvain.—Tr.

Forest and Lake Constance, with her sister Erna and Rosa Guttmann. She read a great deal of Stefan George, Goethe, Gottfried Keller.

Edith began turning her mind to more important things. Among Reinach's notes Edith read: "Everything bears the imprint of God, including time and space." Also, "God, in His mercy, has granted me a new life . . . . Through prayer, I come into contact with the ultimate cause of the world."[2] There are two ways to this realization: the mind and the soul— but the light which shines upon one is the same which illumines the other. The ultimate components of the universe, whose necessity Edith's mind grasped through the influence of her teachers, is what lay ahead of her mental development and prayer. Guided by Husserl and Reinach, her mind arrived at these conclusions, and her soul, enkindled by the example of the Reinachs, received the revelation like a seed about to quicken into life.

Those who knew Edith well are inclined to describe her as somewhat cold and distant. So it may seem at first glance, but if it does, it is because her love of souls was something deeper than mere emotional display. She wanted to lavish on the world that "sympathy" to which Max Scheler had focused

2 J. M. Oesterreicher, *Sept philosophes juifs devant le Christ.* The pupil in question was the future Sister Aldegonde Jaeger-schmidt, OSB.

his attention and research. She expected the same treatment in return, but in a much more profound expression than simply an effusive cordiality. She desired to base her encounter with the world in her love for creation: "The love I encounter in my life," she wrote, "strengthens and develops me, giving me the power to do unheard of things. If the mistrust I sometimes have to contend with paralyzes in me all my creative ability, affection and an understanding willing kindness, on the other hand, bring me such rich treasure that I am able to share it with others without fear of exhausting myself in so doing." When she noticed Husserl's students struggling with his lofty and exceedingly difficult teachings, Edith found the way to express her desire to help others by organizing introductory courses in phenomenology. Someone asked her if it were true she taught philosophy at Freiburg, and she replied, "No. I'm satisfied with running a kindergarten for would-be philosophers." The future Sister Aldegonde Jaegerschmidt saw this in Edith when she described her "knack for teaching" and training pupils "with endless patience, an attentive and quiet generosity. Always friendly, without the least irony or criticism, she welcomed our awkward questions with a calmness, an even temper and dedication, so much so that we would scarcely give her a minute's peace . . . . Untiringly, she nudged us a little further along the foreboding path to intellectual knowledge. The zeal which consumed her won our hearts. We were heady with the sheer joy of learning."

Husserl fell sick in the autumn of 1918, and at his request Edith read him the Bible. Husserl had stepped up to the very threshold of the Faith and spoke as a man of deep religious convictions: "The life of man is only a progression towards God", he said to one of his students. "I have tried to reach this progression towards God without theological proofs, methods or aids—in other words, I tried to reach God without God's help." Edith must have seen the impossibility of such a task. Husserl added, "I tried in one way or another to delete God from my scientific thought so that I might outline a way to Him for those who lack the security of faith in the Church which we have." He clearly saw that "this method of procedure would be disastrous (for him if he) had not a deep attachment to God and belief in Christ to hold on to."

Indeed, Edith was quite far removed from Husserl. During this period, Husserl's philosophy took a turn toward a pure interior experience and a philosophy of the consciousness. It was no longer in touch with the reality of existence which had so attracted Edith.

An obstacle lifted from Edith's path. She returned to Breslau and, in February of 1919, Husserl presented her a kind of "certificate"—a glowing testimony on the quality of her philosophical teachings and a token of his appreciation for all the work she had done for him. As if her new professorship at Göttingen were not enough, Edith completed her psychological projects which were published in the 1922 *Yearbook*. In them she applied her analysis to real-life situations such as weariness, feverishness, and observed these phenomena governed by the mental attitude we take in life. She expressed her deep concern about the meaning of her existence whose secret she had not yet uncovered. This interior duality nourished her psychological experience with riches that examination on other phenomena would not have revealed. Thus she wrote: "I can ardently desire religious faith without receiving it." Also, "Suppose a totally convinced atheist experiments with the existence of God because of a religious experience. He could be totally oblivious of faith while investigating it. He forbids it to act within him, but clings instead to his scientific vision of the world which would shrink before an unchecked faith."[3]

As Scheler, Husserl, Gabriel Marcel in France,

3 *Beiträge zur philosophischen Begründung der Psychologie, Jahrbuch* (1922), Vol. 5.

and Jaspers as well (though in a different way),[4] Edith Stein encountered faith as a *living experience*, as an experience founded on Truth. At this point she broke away from the rationalism of the preceding age. It was not a question of a struggle with concepts or with ideas void of human "meaning": the time when man was reduced to what he "thought" had come to an end. It was finished and done with because such an outlook could give life no real meaning. Suddenly, the life of Faith reappears as Truth in the very center of creation in the lives of men who wanted, certainly, *to think,* but rightly *to think in terms of the whole life.* The same "experience"— if one may call it that—will find a parallel in the second generation of psychoanalysts, Jung for example. They observed faith in their analyses of the living human being, and they looked upon it as a balancing factor and the realization of truth in existence: thus, a psychoanalyst as Jung would come to recognize that the themes of faith (especially Catholicism) best correspond to the interior appeal of the human life.[5]

As we have seen exemplified in her childhood, the mind and soul of Edith Stein were razor-sharp. Husserl read the Bible, saw the "obstacle" but edged

4 cf. *L'Introduction à la Philosophie,* or the *Situation Spirituelle de notre époque.*

5 C. G. Jung, *Psychology and Religion.*

about it. Reinach jumped the hurdle. Edith Stein's keen logic would do the same. Hers was a twofold logic: that of the intellect and soul. If faith, the *explanation* of being, holds the key to the mystery of the universe, her soul had to cleave to it, but it could not unless her intellect had arrived at the same conclusion. Man's existence is a unity; and Edith threw herself into the quest for the whole man.

We readily see that Edith *was living the life of faith already*, and never will "you would not look for me if you had not already found me" find so true a personification as in her. But Edith required both mind and soul to find a common resting place in order that her soul might partake of all arrived at through the mind, so that the mind could verify everything the soul perceived. Which moved which: mind or soul? They both supported and constantly converged one upon the other. Perhaps her mind first realized the exigencies of truth, the necessity of going back to the source of being, but—and this is important to see—her soul had already advanced far into the perception and meditation of the mystery of being.

After her request for a lecturing position at Göttingen was turned down, Edith spent the summer of 1921 with her friend Frau Conrad-Martius and husband at their farm in the Palatinate. Like Edith,

Hedwig Conrad-Martius was one of Husserl's most promising pupils, and their work together united them in deep friendship. Though Hedwig Martius was a Protestant, her library contained more than one Catholic book, among which was *The Life of St. Teresa of Avila, written by herself.* One evening in that summer of 1921, Edith was alone at the farm and picked up the autobiography of St. Teresa. She read it through all night long, and in the early morning finished it, whereupon she exclaimed, "There is Truth!"

We do not consider this to be a premature enlightenment. Her mind had been prepared for it in advance through Scheler and Reinach. It was rather a coincidence all at once perceived—a kind of illumination, naturally—between what Edith had felt developing in her and the spiritual experience of the Saint of Carmel.

Frau Conrad-Martius described the kind of life they led together at the farm: "We wanted to live as much in the deeply-rooted spiritual ideal of poverty as possible. I remember one day we were carrying coal, when Professor Koyré came to pay us a visit. He was beside himself at the sight of women doing such heavy work. After nightfall we were much too exhausted to discuss philosophy and, apart from the few times our friends came to see us, we usually spent our evenings either darning and sewing ...

or retiring early." Frau Conrad-Martius adds, "She suffered a set-back in her development when, though she had a Christian outlook on life, she had not directly attacked the problem of faith." She goes on to say that Edith "was a good and wise woman with unflagging devotion..., she remained quite secretive and quiet.... She always looked abstracted as though absorbed in an unbroken meditation.... We were the closest of friends, but I know nothing of any consequence which I can say about her interior evolution."[6]

Her "unbroken meditation"—a meditation so profound, so "existential"—so enveloped the whole of existence that it could not be shared with others. Her reading of St. Teresa was but the consequence of her "meditation". We have a text written during this "meditative" period which appeared after her conversion in 1922:[7] "I am making plans for the future," Edith wrote, "and am arranging my immediate life accordingly. But I am deeply convinced that something is looming in the offing which will upset all my projects. I mean the true and living faith which I still refuse to assent to, which I prevent from becoming active within me." She, the created

6 cf. "Letters of Frau Conrad-Martius" in *Edith Stein*.

7 That Edith Stein wrote this text during this particular period is verified by a well-informed witness, Marie Biemas, *Katolische Frauenbildung* (November, 1952).

one, had been summoned, had heard His voice and knew that it was directed to her personally. Faith quickened within her and she felt the existence of the total and infinite Creator—how could she, then, still balk at taking the final step? Such a refusal of truth was so unlike her. We shall understand her position if we picture her waiting until she had become absolutely certain that her whole being could accept the faith for her to make that final plunge totally, in complete certitude and perfect understanding of the final "Yes", that *Fiat* to the whole body of revealed truth.

This text continues in such a way as to leave absolutely no doubt about this period of a truly spiritual experience: "There exists a state of repose in God, a total suspension of all mental activity in which one can neither make plans or decisions, in which one can do nothing, but in which, having consigned all things to the divine will, one surrenders entirely to his destiny. *I have experienced this state somewhat, following an experience which, exceeding all my own abilities, totally consumed my spiritual energies and divested me of all possible action. Compared to the cessation of activity rising from lack of strength, repose in God is something at once new and indomitable. Previously, it was the silence of death, but this gave way to a feeling of intimate security and surcease from all anxiety,* obligation and responsibility in relation to action. And while I gave myself up to this feeling, *a new life began little by little to pour into me* and—without forcing my will— urged me again to action. This vital onrush seems to come from an activity and a force which is not mine and without doing violence to what is mine, becomes active within me. The only condition for such a spiritual rebirth seems to be a certain receptivity which is at the very basis of the individual who is aloof from any kind of psychical mechanism."

Ten years later, Bergson said that the mystical soul falls silent, as though listening to a voice calling it, then immediately surrenders itself before it. Bergson said the soul does not directly *perceive* the *force* which overpowers it, but only senses its undefinable presence. The soul of a great mystic does not come to a standstill in ecstacy, but it is a *repose*, though while waiting for another upcharge, movement continues in this excitement.[8] Is this not what Edith felt going on inside?

She still refused Baptism and even went so far as to believe that she "refused to consent to the Faith". However, by this time she was so committed to the world of grace and faith—infinite grace—that grace was working within her *per speculum et in œnigmate*.

8 Henri Bergson, *Two Sources of Morality and Religion.*

Because she had actually *arrived* at faith, can we not say that during the long silence between her encounter with Reinach's texts and the day she requested Baptism, she underwent the "trials"—the dark night of the senses and the soul—which St. John of the Cross described? We know nothing about this, but we are inclined to think she did. The page quoted above does bring to mind the "prayer of quietude" which St. Teresa placed at the beginning of the contemplative life. Another certainty is that in the year preceding her decisive step, Edith Stein sacrificed something very dear to her so that she could "keep her heart undivided".

... The night drew to a close. Finishing her reading of St. Teresa, Edith Stein set out that very morning for town to buy a small catechism and a missal. God had finally granted her what for many months she asked by a prayer so typical of her: "My thirst for truth was my only prayer" and also by her soul's attention constantly focused on the Eucharist.[9] Henceforth, Edith could say with Teresa: "When the Lord fills us with great favors, the virtues become so alive, and love so informed, that one cannot conceal the effects of this divine action ...." Real

9 Frau Conrad-Martius thought Edith Stein assisted at Mass daily from that very night of her encounter with St. Teresa. She also accompanied Frau Martius to the Temple.

graces shine in us regardless of ourselves, and they always are beneficial to others. That is why the Bridegroom openly tells us: "He has made Charity spring up in me."

Edith pored over her little catechism and missal, and one morning, after Mass, she followed the priest into the sacristy and asked him to baptize her.

Edith was received into the Church on January 1, 1922, the Feast of the Circumcision.[10] She spoke her Latin responses loudly and fervently, and Frau Conrad-Martius observed that "the most beautiful thing of all was her childlike happiness". Edith found her source in the Intellect and came home to her Creator: the love dwelling in her soul responded to the searchings of her mind.

10 In the private Chapel of the Bishop of Speyer.

EDITH
STEIN

4 EDITH'S STUDY OF THOMISTIC REALISM AND HER SUBSEQUENT REJECTION OF EXISTENTIALISTIC SUBJECTIVISM

It is quite likely that Edith realized her progression toward Baptism long before she requested it. A longing such as hers would compel one to go all the way to a total commitment in union with Him who had given so much. She received Holy Communion on the day of her baptism—and daily from then on. The Bishop of Speyer confirmed her and she selected Canon Schwind as her spiritual director.

Edith suffered an immense heartache in the midst of her great joy, knowing she would have to tell her mother of the conversion. Choosing not to delay over the matter, she went to Breslau, and kneeling before her she said, "Mother, I am a Catholic." The stoical old woman wept and Edith wept with her. To soften the impact of such a blow, Edith lived with her mother for several months, attending the Synagogue with her as in the past, but now she read the Psalms in an entirely new light.

Edith had to get back to work once again, and Canon Schwind located a teaching position for her at the Dominican convent school in Speyer. There she taught German grammar and literature, living the life of a religious at the school for eight years (1922-1931). The nuns gave her a small room within the convent itself. It was plainly furnished with a bed, closet, shelves, a dressing-table and straight-backed chairs. Here she could follow the convent life, attending Mass the first thing in the morning. Her real life had begun at last. At first she had no other cares except the satisfaction of an insatiable intellectual curiosity. She had attained the God so long sought after and daily performed the mission He entrusted her with. She prayed and received the Sacraments. What more could she desire?

Edith was a good and conscientious professor, devoted to her students. She enjoyed seasoning her classes with a great deal of humor. She lived an interior life, eating and sleeping very little and spending long hours at prayer—her prayerful attitude astounded those who saw her then, upright as a statue with a distant and immobile expression on her face. Her students thought she was a little dis-

1 Edith observed the Jewish fasts.

tant and her teaching quite lofty, and the inspector who checked up on Edith reprimanded her for not using the new teaching methods which incorporated more student participation in the classroom. It grieved her to think she had done less than she ought.

Her life in Speyer was troubled, for the noble gift granted her would take second place to nothing. How could she not help but be wholly absorbed in the great blessing of faith given to her in the form of a continual presence? It was *her* faith, *her* presence with God. Still, she realized the need for more. She talked about entering the Carmel, but her careful director would not hear of it. She was ready for the contemplative life—in fact, she was already a contemplative, but Canon Schwind deemed it wiser for her to go on living as she had. Edith impressed those around her as being physically present with them, but mentally abstracted from them.

She eventually made a great sacrifice by relinquishing her philosophical studies. Although she did not seem to regret it, we think it incredible to imagine a mind such as Edith's at least not suffering inwardly from not *serving*, because her mind and soul were so bound together and their development so parallel. Her mind's desire to serve was no empty intellectual pride—it wanted to serve God, to unite

with the Lord in whom it found the meaning of
the existence of the universe.

During her spare time, Edith translated the
Letters and *Journal* of Cardinal Newman with all
the care and precision she devoted to everything.
Father Przywara, who met Edith through Canon
Schwind, immediately sensed the special fibre of
her mind and soul, as if translating one of the
greatest converts of the modern era were not a
thing of mere chance, he touched right to the heart
of her problems when he counseled her to study
St. Thomas. She asked him how to begin investigating
the Church's philosophy, and he replied, "Begin with
St. Thomas right away. Don't bother with manuals
or commentaries." This remarkable Jesuit saw the
"Angelic Doctor" would satisfy Edith's mind already
attuned to the profound logic of being and the
Source of Being. Just as St. Thomas had supported
and directed the great mystics of the Carmel—John
of the Cross and Teresa,—so also he was about to
influence Edith by showing her intellect what the
Saint of Avila had already taught her soul.

To get her involved in Thomism, Father Przywara advised Edith to translate St. Thomas' *Quaesti-
ones Disputatae de Veritate* into German. Quite a
difficult undertaking, it brought her much discour-
agement, and some men of letters—Joseph Piper for
one—upbraided her for occasional obscurities and

ambiguities. But Edith tackled something that went far beyond the mechanics of translating when she confronted modern thought with the Church's ancient thought, and from this juncture came her own work entitled *Husserl's Phenomenology and the Philosophy of St. Thomas Aquinas.*

She understood that the essential Thomistic intuition had actually prompted her throughout her intellectual life: the existence of the universe is an incontrovertible reality, and we are in its milieu; it exists for us, and we for it; the intellect is nothing if not the "capturer" of being. Behind the existence of the universe, animating and sustaining it, is an infinite intellect which makes us aware of the universe so that we can interpret and recognize it, discover its meaning, and thereby the reason for our own existence.

Edith was particularly excited by the chapter in *De Veritate* which treats on the way God knows both the universe and Himself: all things are totally and absolutely present to Him. He has no need of encountering anything in actual experience as we do or undergoing the slow and nebulous logical progression from effect to cause. In God, being and knowledge are one and the same: He is all that He knows, He knows all that is, and only what He knows exists.

Edith perceived the universal presence of God

in the existence of the world from the very outset
of the intellectual search that culminated in her
accepting the Catholic Faith. This illumination was
in keeping with her first philosophical thoughts. The
Faith she found filled her entirely with certainty,
but we should not be taken aback in learning that her
religious faith did not set all things up in their
proper perspectives. Perhaps she was not really
a Thomist at first; maybe she assigned too great a
value on the will in the development of knowledge;
she certainly did confuse theology and philosophy
by making philosophy too dependent on theology
and nearly subordinating all true knowledge to the
Faith. Later, she came to sense the "balance" of the
"eternal philosophy". Irregardless of this confusion
between the two, the essential point she grasped at
once: *ens, verum, bonum convertuntur*—"Being, the
true, the good are convertible." All that exists is
true, good and beautiful, and outside the immense
realm of creation there is nothing.

She embraced this truth with all her might, and
it answered one of her earliest questions. It was the
answer to the misery befallen her world, and shortly
to utterly devastate it: as the idea of an objective
good, a natural law imposing rights and duties upon
creatures is lost sight of, the shadow of *nothingness*,
an empty void, spreads out over the globe. Dostoyevsky and Nietzsche, two opposites, come together

at this point: "If there be no God, then all things are to be allowed", Dostoyevsky made one of his characters exclaim, and Nietzsche resounded with "God is dead." Then, "all things are to be allowed" and a great despair will settle over the world: nothing will have meaning, and all human acts will only echo the "emptiness" of the rest of the world. The "existential" novelists, borrowing these conclusions from one branch of existentialism, chanted this mournful dirge.

All her life Edith knew the mind revealed existence, but if she knew that—and this would explain her early confusion between rational philosophy and theology enlightened by Faith—if she knew that, it had been initially enlightened by her love for the world to which she readily opened her heart. In that intense, clearsighted love for the world, she ascended to the stature of Husserl himself, for in that love she condemned the entire subjectivistic universe that admittedly depended upon itself in the most hideous of egoisms—intellectual pride. As soon as all things are referred to the "subject", philosophy itself becomes an impossibility, and that is why modern rationalism is at an impasse. Edith wrote, "Through this means it is impossible to get away from the sphere of immanence to return back to the objectivity from which Husserl started out, and which he realized the necessity of protecting.

It is impossible to get back to a truth and a reality void of all subjective reality." Never will "the mind in search of truth" be able to consent to "identifying existence with an automanifestative process of the consciousness." Also, one "makes God Himself a relative something", and this is the most glaring difference between phenomenology such as Edith knew and Catholic philosophy. The first is "egocentric", the second "theocentric."[2]

In Husserl's work Edith understood the *projection* of the human being beyond his exclusive, individual "egocentric" world—she interpreted him correctly. But it was Husserl—a study easily enough bears this out, and it is an almost incontrovertible fact—who receded into a renewal of subjectivism. Edith went her way and surpassed her teacher, going so far as to show how Thomism, the most traditional philosophy of the Church—designated by Leo XIII, Pius X and Pius XII as the natural philosophy of Christianity—answers the questions of the most "modern" minds expressed in phenomenology and existentialism.

The philosophy of St. Thomas avoids getting ensnared in the endless debate of post-Cartesian rationalism and idealism, in initially positing a foundation for intellectual knowledge in experimen-

2 Edith Stein herself used these terms.

tal perception as perceived through the senses. The first step for the human mind is to accept a real existing world outside itself. It recognizes that there are actually beings, that they are permanent and that our senses, though they do not reveal the essence of the world to us, at least do not deceive us in what they do impart about the exterior world outside the mind. In this way, we conclude there really is a table here, that a solid is a solid, a form remains like to itself so long as other internal or external forces do not change it, etc.

Childish? Perhaps it may seem puerile at first glance. But its acceptance is the only way to get out of the mind and into the world. It is the only way to escape the snags of solipsism, the only way to end up with having something *to think,* reason about ... and to act upon.

Phenomenology used a word found in the Medieval Christian philosophy and it was sneered at by 19th century rationalism: *intentionality.* How does the mind grasp what it comes into contact with? How can we assimilate and assume something experienced in the world outside the mind? How is it that we can distinguish order in the midst of chaos? We do not pause to think about such things because we are accustomed—too accustomed—to accept the "operations" of the mind and the "information" it gives us, and yet this is one of the very greatest mysteries: the primary and basic correspondence between the forms of the world and the workings of the mind through which the intellect "captures" existence. In the mind's attention there is a profound *intention* that corresponds to what the world offers it to interpret.

The meaning of *intentionality* has been much discussed among the Phenomenologists and Thomists, and we shall not go into it here. Let it suffice to say that from the time she began to examine St. Thomas and found the intellectual atmosphere she had been searching for, Edith Stein conceived of the intentionality of the mind in the way St. Thomas did.

However, on another point Edith's starting position in philosophy was not quite orthodox. She wrote first that the foundation, the departure for Thomistic philosophy was Faith. In reality, it was a natural experience—her encounter with the world—for Edith Stein. She set Husserl's idea that "the unifying point of departure is the transcendentally purified consciousness" in opposition to St. Thomas' "God and His relation to creation". Soon she came to see that the true Thomistic foundation for knowledge is the relationship between creatures, and it follows that the mind is made to know, since it comes into contact with creation and thereby results in a thorough knowledge of these creatures and their universe. The intellect perceives the necessity of God and Creator.

Again, let us not be surprised at the direction of her thought: Faith revealed to her the meaning of the universe, and in a sense it was only natural that she make faith the cornerstone and assign it the primary place in her intellect as she did in her life.

The progression of Edith's thought is extremely interesting. As far as she was concerned there was not, and never could be, on the one hand a philosopher who continued to think according to the laws of philosophy, and on the other a person led to conversion by experiences from life and meditation on beings and their spiritual significance. Everything met and became united in her soul, and her mind was indissolubly bound to her soul. Her intellect moved her soul. As a philosopher, she perceived the imperfection of the world and saw the necessity for a Being more existent than all creation which is but a manifestation of this Being. Hers was truly a *philosophical* conversion, the conversion of a *philosophical mind* which advanced from the first stages to the realization that to be fully a human being, the mind and soul must be inseparable. Is it too much to say that this is her own message which Providence entrusted to her in the age of phenomenologists and existentialists?

She was born to ride the waves of existential phenomenology and draw inferences from it; to show from the failure of the best philosophies of the age—Rationalism and Idealism—that one must begin with the primary truths of the existence of an exterior world and the ability of the mind to know this world exterior to itself. She resolved these conclusions to their ultimate consequences. Philosophy can only lead to metaphysics, to the knowledge of being, to ontology, and ontology can only lead to God. No knowledge of being failed to discover in the center of the world what Edith discovered there.

EDITH STEIN

5 THE WAY OF COMPLETE SURRENDER

Edith lived a voluntary monastic life at the convent in Speyer. The radiance of her interior life drew people's attention and they came to her for advice and consolation. Edith's somewhat distant personality gave way to a warm tenderness that let her become one with the trials of other people. She was able to suffer with them and help them as only the saints whose lives center upon Christ are capable of doing.[1] "She gave solace to souls that priests and spiritual directors considered lost."

Her students, philosophy, spiritual guidance and most of all, prayer, were quite enough to keep her constantly active, but deep within her soul Edith wanted to give herself up entirely to the contemplation of the Lord who called her. Father Przywara, waiting for the moment when he was sure of her vocation—the Church is indeed wise—advised Edith

[1] Testimony of a Dominican religious from Speyer, in H. C. Graef, *The Scholar and the Cross.*

to make several retreats with the Benedictines at
Beuron.

Edith spent her summer vacation at home with
her mother. She continued to be the same attentive,
loving and beloved daughter. But there grew a bar-
rier between mother and daughter—a chasm all the
more insurmountable in that they loved each other
and wanted to either win over or at least come to
understand the other. On top of this, Edith lived
in the midst of her whole intensely Jewish family
which did not understand her motives, and when
she tried to explain them even to her best friends,
they hesitated to follow her for countless reasons—
sometimes just to keep peace in their own families.
The atmosphere stifled Edith. Beuron would surely
be doubly a harbor of peace.

Father Przywara was making his own plans for
Edith's future. Of late, Edith had taken interest in
the German feminist movement. Why not get her
to devote a part of her intelligence and apostolic
zeal to the Catholic Woman's project? And so, in
1928, Edith launched into a new activity which
began with a conference to the Catholic women
teachers of Bavaria—a series of talks on the Church's
views of the woman's role in life.[2]

2 Collected in French under the heading *La femme et sa
destinée,* (Amiot-Dumont, publishers).

Edith was by now familiar enough with the Thomistic approach to strike right at the heart of the problem with "Is there a woman's nature?" Before knowing how to educate "the woman", or deciding what kind of life she ought live, one must know what "woman" really is. Edith Stein then noted that one's actions cannot be considered separate from one's soul. Now a woman by her very nature is meant to be wife and mother, and so no education can prescind from this vocation. "It is not the body alone", she affirmed, "which has a different structure, and not only are there many various individual physiological functions, but her whole physical make-up is different. There are different relations between a woman's body and soul, different connections between mind and sensibility . . . ." Because she is as though *made for another* by her very essence, a woman "will find her strength in the intuition of the concrete and the living", she is called to "grasp the concrete in its particularity".

Between 1920 and 1935 Germany reeled under the impact of internal disorder: the post-Bismarckian empire collapsed; the revolutions from 1918 to 1920, economic chaos and unemployment crises. These not only upset the nation's political stability, but wreaked havoc with German family unity as well. Abruptly and brutally Germany passed from the dominant Prussian Protestant Puritanism, which the

Wilhelmian government had inculcated into the fibre of the empire, to an erotic anarchy against morality which, though it did not directly influence every family, gave rise to many formidable problems and questioned the accepted laws of moral living. Amidst this disarray of thinking, Edith voiced more than the Church's tradition, for in a sense they were only secondary to her. Edith was first and foremost a young Jewish university professor immersed in the activity of youth. She went out on many long nature-outings which so deeply characterized this generation of the *Wandervögel*. She belonged to this generation and was herself a "bird-of-passage" in her questioning of all the ideas and ways of life of her era. Moreover, she was acquainted with the psychology of her times. It was her first specialty. She understood psychoanalysis and all the schools of scientific and experimental psychology.

Her conferences took her throughout Germany and all its colorful regions and because of her immense background, Edith brought the girls and women who listened to her not the mouthings of a classic wisdom, but the discoveries of intellectual experience and all the answers which modern psychology had to offer.

Edith's investigations taught her a great deal more than woman's subordination to man, and she denounced as a "deprivation proper to women" the concept of a life bound to man "by fetters of servitude" and "the wilting of a woman's mind in the physico-sensual life". Some of her work on the "subordination to sex" are strikingly relevant in the light of eroticism. No woman, she maintained, will find herself by simply being a "rebel slave". If it be true that "the meaning of a specifically womanly existence cannot be understood merely by relationships existing between men and women", and if the role of the mother is essential, still neither of these relationships help us to fully understand all that a woman is. A woman is no more meant *for* man than for herself. They both have a place in God's plans.

In May of that year Edith was compelled to show "the purpose of woman's formation". Just as there is an "imitation of Christ" for all mankind, so too there would be an "imitation of Mary" for women.

We must not think for a minute that Edith lived in the rarified atmosphere of abstract ideas. Quite to the contrary, she gleaned lessons which she could apply to the most concrete facets of life, especially when she evolved an *ethic* of feminine professions. And because she had thoroughly examined the "womanly type" fenced in between the limits of the sin of Eve and the virginity of Mary, she dealt with the most concrete of beings. What a union between the loftiest and simplest we find here: "The inclinations of a woman for what is living and personal" can be led "in the wrong direction": "to desire spending all her time excessively on herself and others" or "taking too much interest in others through sheer curiosity and indiscreet prying into their lives".

Edith betrayed her inmost self with her writings on the contemplative life. Try as she may not to rely on her own experience, Edith's very words betrayed the secrets of her contemplative life, and this is to be expected, for constant attendance in choir, long hours of meditation before the Eucharist, and unending prayer cannot but reveal themselves.

"Losing oneself completely in a loving surrender to God, allowing one's own life to come to an end to make room for God's life, is the motive and principle of the religious life." And Edith enumerated these loves—a love springing from compassion, protection, and a love rising out of participation (which "mourns with those who are in mourning and rejoices with those who are joyful"). All these loves are "at the disposal of every creature so that it might become what the Father desires it should". In the heart of such a love, a woman's vocation is revealed: "To surrender oneself to another through love, to become entirely the property of another, and to possess this other wholly—this is the deepest longing of a woman's heart."

Who, then, could "receive the surrender, the oblation, of a creature in such a way that its soul will not be lost, but saved?" Who, but God? And who "can abandon himself to us, filling our whole being by doing so, without losing anything of himself?" Who, but God?

Neither a woman's vocation nor love are wholly realized except in the total giving of herself to God: "Complete surrender, the aim of the religious life, is at the same time the only adequate fulfillment of a woman's aspirations."

Not all women have to enter the strictly religious life, but they must "in every way become the hand-maids of the Lord, after the example of the Mother of God". When she spoke to the women of Germany, Edith never once hesitated to mention details of daily life to show how great love is expressed in the observance of little things. She saw—and admired—her mother's life, and it remained a blessed example for her to follow. What the Synagogue produced, so could the Church, but the Law had to be made more loving. She always insisted that, in the religious life as well as life in the world, "the average must not be contented just with the ideal".

But, if her soul abounded in such a great love, and if she was able to perceive God in all things, then what held her back from reaching out to grasp the "ideal"? All her attention was focused on these ideals, and to keep them alive within her, Edith looked to the saints for examples to follow. She was especially fond of St. Elizabeth of Hungary. Elizabeth knew all the joy and fulfillment of a great love. She could bask in the glory of her throne and a glittering reign, and yet, in the midst of all that happiness and fame, her first concern was for the downtrodden, the starving, and all those whom the nobles at court wanted her to ignore. She wanted to do more for the God she loved, and she accepted the will of God when He took her husband during the Crusades. She forsook her wealth and consecrated herself entirely to the Lord by becoming one of His poorest servants when she openly adopted the Rule of St. Francis which she had long followed secretly.[3]

What more shining example than this? Edith Stein called upon her listeners to out-do the wonders of the Saints themselves. The very source of light glows behind all their brilliant deeds. Among her conferences on St. Elizabeth of Hungary, there is one page in particular which best explains where the little Jewish philosopher of Breslau had been heading now for quite some time. She depicted Elizabeth as animated by the love and pursuit of

3 Edith Stein, *La Femme et sa destinée*, (French translation, p. 107).

the Lord. "When her parents allowed her to go about as she pleased, the Lord went with her, even into distant and strange lands. Because she knew He dwelt in the castle's chapel, she felt drawn to that place . . . . There she felt at home . . . . No one is so faithful as He." Such accents do not err. Elizabeth was much like the Great St. Teresa, and Edith was like them both, wholly magnetized, entirely drawn towards Him, seeing that the world of color is but a reflection of Him, and having no joy and peace except when in His presence.

Even then, Edith fully possessed her religious vocation, but the road to the Carmel was closed to her: Dom Walzer, the Benedictine whose advice she sought during her retreats at Beuron Abbey, and Father Przywara as well, kept her in the world. Who was more qualified than Edith, an eminent philosopher and Jewish convert, to tell the women of Germany what she did? That was her vocation and, when she spoke of Elizabeth of Hungary, the routine of daily living, or the primary duty of obedience, she spoke from actual experience. True, the road to the Carmel was still closed to her, but she found the very heart of existence where knowledge and the soul are intimately united. She found the relationship between the natural and the supernatural, of a nature not totally itself if it gives itself up entirely to the "natural" plane without being nourished by the supernatural to which one's deepest nature is attracted.

We cannot discuss everything she taught about the religious formation of children. This is a most important topic because it is rooted in concise philosophical insight and the Thomistic vision of the human condition: "Faith is not imagination," she wrote, "it is an intellectual apprehension. A fully developed faith is one of the profoundest acts of the personality .... The emotions are certainly valuable aids and stimulating forces urging the will to give assent, but if the intellect and will are not called upon to produce the greatest part of the effort, one will not develop a life of genuine and full faith."

Centered upon the loftiest philosophical and theological grounds, Edith's vision of creation permitted her to give those attending her conferences a way to avoid the passing fancies of the moment, without becoming oblivious to the needs of the age. She could advance right to the center of the problem, because she gauged its depth with the measuring rod of doctrine: "The gentle weapons of psychology and esthetics are pledged to fight against the real forces of temptation and passion, to the finish. Only the fully developed power of the Mystery can achieve victory on this front." Edith also stressed that "A good part of the Christian formation consists in learning to lead one's life in communion with the

Lord", and one must "strike up the flames of enthusiasm in one's heart" for the ideal which makes a woman's life "the symbol of the mysterious union which Christ contracted with His Church and humanity redeemed".

This most modern of psychological technicians is truly an excellent example for us to follow. She did not disdain, in any manner whatsoever, the methods and means which psychology put at our disposal to help people regain control of themselves and advance to God. But, because she was also an experienced philosopher, and because she became more and more a theologian, she knew, as she said herself, that human nature is not sufficient unto itself, and that only the total Spiritual Life can respond to nature. The total Spiritual Life alone, can come face-to-face with the problems of nature. Unlike many, Edith saw how impossible it was to give children first what is called a "human" education, and then to wait until the "age of reason" before bringing divine life into their souls. As an experienced psychologist, she knew that the human being is fully human from the moment of birth and until death—potentially, at least, in the qualities of imagination, sentiment, emotion and reason, but that they only awaken slowly, though they are not less present to the human person right from birth. She knew, as she taught, that the "divine force living within us" must nourish the whole being every moment—and one must have recourse to this power even in professional life . . . .

How she would have liked to give herself up entirely to this force and divine presence! Already devoted to it, she lived a semi-conventual life at Speyer, made retreats and visits to Beuron, and all the while, that same force guided her during her lecturing career. She aspired to more, but her spiritual directors did not recommend it, and, faithful to them, she obeyed. Because they considered she would be more useful and influential, Edith sadly consented to resign from the private boarding school at Speyer, on Easter of 1931, and seek a chair of philosophy at the University of Freiburg.

She lived almost that whole summer with her mother at Breslau. The atmosphere was very oppressive there. Her sister Rosa wanted to become baptized, but neither of them dared break their aged mother's heart again. Edith, who never ceased praying for her mother, hesitated, but her presence in Breslau helped to bolster Rosa up. For the time being, at least, their mutual love for their mother made them spare fresh heartaches.

No answer came from Freiburg, and Edith applied for another position, whereupon they offered her a professorship in philosophy at Breslau. Frau Stein did not flinch at the sight of her daughter teaching Catholic philosophy in the city of her birth. She needed Edith with her, now more than ever. Though so great a love as Edith's did not conquer the Synagogue, it did, however, break down the barriers.

During these months without work, Edith wrote a long tract on St. Thomas' potency and act. She carried on a voluminous correspondence, answering all who came to her for help and advice. Their numbers constantly swelled—women who attended her conferences, former pupils. She led them to the Psalms, advising them by the sacred texts.

At Breslau, she felt the lack of liturgical life: "The silent liturgy is my lot here. We can, of course, receive as much of this as we need, but it is only when I shall again live the liturgy in all its fullness that I shall feel how much of it I have been deprived of. When I left Speyer, I knew it would be quite difficult to live outside the cloister, but I had no idea how difficult." Who can still hold Edith back from what she was called to?

Her plans at Breslau did not materialize. In the spring of 1922, Edith accepted the lectureship at the Institute of Educational Theory at Münster. There, she could divide her time between feminine pedagogy and philosophy. During these years, Edith read Gertrude von Le Fort's book *The Song at the Scaffold,* which influenced Bernanos to write his

Dialogues des Carmelites. She waited for her destiny to unfold into total prayer and sacrifice. Though it was not yet the proper time, she set out on the last lap of her journey, already in the unitive way of prayer.

EDITH STEIN

6 HER PERSONAL PRAYER DURING THE GATHERING STORM

"She spoke little, but her every word was filled with meaning, for they sprang from the depths of silence and prayer", wrote a companion of Edith Stein.[1] She added, "How can one ever forget the sober glances, unspeakably sad, she cast upon the Crucified, the King of the Jews, when she saw the constantly increasing threat of more violent racial persecutions. One day, I heard her say, 'Oh, how much my people must suffer before they become converted!' And the thought flashed through my mind that Edith was offering herself up to God for the conversion of Israel."

We do not know, there is no reliable testimony or writing to tell us that Edith really was "offering

[1] Sister Aldegonde Jaegerschmidt, who knew Edith during her school days, later became a convert from Protestantism and entered the Benedictine convent of St. Lioba, at Freiburg in Brisgau, where Edith made several visits.

herself up" for her Israelite brothers and sisters, but we are inclined to think that Edith's piety had not yet taken so clearly defined a course. She was aspiring to the union of her whole being with the Lord, and it was, indeed, a total offering which she had attained: an offering *already* realized, she was *sacrificed*, totally. Sacrificed without stint, offered up in so intense a union with the divine will, that her sacrifice was fully *made* for all. We may readily believe that, in her life of union in contemplative prayer, Edith had had the suffering of her people often before the eyes of her soul. And she united all the misery about to befall her people to her own offering, and brought it to Him whom she loved; for, at the very basis of everything about her, even her prayer, love governed all.

The text we quoted from Sister Aldegonde notes the two opposite poles around which Edith's life would revolve: prayer and suffering for her Jewish brethren, and the persecutions of Hitler which would swallow her up and bring her to death.

Already, the expressions of her personal piety had taken shape. The girl, who remained motionless so long before the Eucharist, waited for the grace she already possessed, and whose presence she wished to make increasingly more welcome. Her prayer and devotion were, above all, responsive to grace. Was there anything more in addition to this?

Among the papers written during the period she taught at Münster, Edith called souls to more of a "general disposition" rather than to develop "precise qualities". "We cannot acquire this condition by an effort of our own will; it must be the workings of grace. But we can, and must, open ourselves to grace." How? "By denying our own will completely, and surrendering only to the will of God, making our whole soul receptive to re-casting in His divine hands. Thus, silence and self-forgetfulness are bound together." She was not yet a Carmelite when she spoke these words, but hers was the spirit of St. John of the Cross and St. Teresa of Avila. Edith sketched an outline for daily living: If we rush headlong, throwing ourselves into the duties and cares of the day, then we must stop and say to ourselves, "Wait! None of this must bother me now ... The Mystery of Redemption is what matters here, and not myself. I am allowed to share in this Mystery, *to be cleansed by it and to rejoice in it*, and I am permitted to offer myself, and all my actions and sufferings, together with the spotless Victim on the altar. And when the Lord comes to me in Holy Communion, I may ask Him, like St. Teresa, 'What do you want of me, Lord?' *and after this silent dialogue, I shall do what He bids me* ... Because my soul will have gone out of itself, it will be able to penetrate into the divine life. The Lord will have enkindled in me the fire of charity, compelling me to share this fire of love with others ... The soul will clearly see the next stretch of road ahead. It will not see very far, but when it has travelled that distance, a whole new horizon will open up before it ...."

What a serene abandonment these words contain, and how in keeping with the tranquil humility of this little way of simple abandon is the royal road of Contemplation ... Edith had entered into this "silent dialogue" some while back, and she did not have to look for the life of the soul she described, because it was her own.

Germany, in the meanwhile, flared up all around her. The Weimar Republic tottered on unsteady ground, and unemployment, misery, humiliation and political passions heaped up coals on this fire which the Nazis fanned into an inferno.

In the spring of 1932, when Edith accepted a tutorial position at the Educational Institute in Münster, Germany began that chain of events which one year later would bring Hitler to power. On May 10, Marshal Hindenburg was elected President of the German Republic, and on June 1, Von Papen formed the government. On the fourteenth of June, Von Papen introduced the measure taken by the government of the Catholic Chancellor, Brüning, dissolving Hitler's SS and SA troopers. On July 31, the elections gave Hitler an overwhelming majority in the Reich-stag.

But Edith went her own way: "One must find peace . . . . Nothing must deter us from containing ourselves and from fleeing to the Lord. He is ever present . . . ." If in the evening we are dissatisfied with ourselves, "Let us take ourselves for what we are . . . that we shall be able to find repose in Him."

We should really be mistaken in assuming that Edith, absorbed in her interior life, was indifferent to things going on in the world. In one of her earlier works, she spoke of the "experience of a vanquished people", and one who "would share in the immense and unfathomable suffering encircling this people, finds himself overwhelmed by it". The swelling wave of hatred was about to crash down upon *her* people, the Jewish People, the people of her mother, brothers and sisters. Edith was always one of these people. Dom Feuling relates that, going to Montmartre with her and Koyré, whom she met in Germany, and who was sent to teach at the Sorbonne, he heard them speaking of the Jewish People as "we". Edith's conversion had not destroyed the bonds of solidarity which bound her to her people. And besides, how could she feel freed from them when, every time she returned to Breslau, and again, when in the year before, during her long stay at home, she saw her mother grieved by her daughter's apostasy?

By no means did she live isolated from the world, and if the truth be known, she felt all the more intensely united to those who suffered when she prayed.

"She hid her interior life," said the Director of the Educational Institute of Münster, where Edith spent the year of 1932. "One had to guess at it or discover it indirectly", but "one could almost feel it when watching her at prayer". The Abbot of Beuron, after affirming that "her interior life was simple and straightforward ... a soul lifted up to the heights, wholly illumined ...," went on to say that the very "idea of affecting a pose" was utterly alien to her. On the contrary, "she did not want extraordinary graces or ecstacies ... She desired only to be with God, as though her presence in a holy place (the Abbey) assured her of a proximity with the mysteries of faith she could find nowhere else ... Just as her body, fixed in an almost total state of immobility, so also her mind dwelt peacefully in the loving contemplation of God, in the joy of our Lord."

Edith longed for the day when she could enter the Carmel. There, she would be joined continually in the prayer of the Church: "It seemed," wrote the Abbot of Beuron, "that the liturgy, austere in both its length and brevity, had become an indispensable food for her." But there too, Edith would embark upon a path where even her fondness for the spiritual would not be wholly satisfied; for she would have the Office with the Benedictines in all its fullness, but "souls such as hers, once seized by the spirit of the absolute, can only embrace a more singular form of religious life, because the desire quickened in her by the inspiration of the Holy Spirit, would always beg for more."[2]

The events that followed were in the hands of Providence. On January 30, 1933, Hitler became Chancellor of the Reich, and on February 27, the Reichstag was burned: two days earlier, Edith gave her last lecture at the Educational Institute of Münster. For some time previous to this, she had to curtail her activities by ending her conferences outside of the Institute, where she was observed. One of her pupils did not bother to hide the fact that she was a follower of Hitler, and she openly displayed her copy of *Mein Kampf*. Edith encouraged her students to form anti-Nazi groups, and though the general Jewish boycott was not decided upon until April, intolerance constantly increased in the teaching profession, and the inevitable time came when Edith could no longer teach.

2 Testimony by Dom Walzer, Abbot of Beuron. Cf. Sister Teresia de Spiritu Sancto, *Edith Stein*, (Part II, Chapter II).

Edith had foreseen this new trial coming, and we might ask ourselves if this really was a trial? It freed her for the Carmel. Her real trial came in seeing the unbridled hatred of men. It was unbearable for her to think of the new sufferings befallen her aged mother, her brothers and sisters in Breslau; it was insupportable for Edith to think that the world had scorned the word of God and rejected Christ's grace.

Edith spent Christmas Eve of 1932—her last in the world—in an Ursuline convent, and one of the religious reports: "On Christmas Eve she joined with us in singing Matins; then we went to rest for an hour until midnight. When I returned to the Church I found her still kneeling motionless in the same position as we had left her; she then sang the Office of Lauds with us. When I asked her later whether she had not been weary, her eyes lit up and she replied: 'How could one grow weary on this night.' "[3]

Two months before (October), she gave her last conference at Aachen for the Catholic Women's League where she learned "to what extent the world had become a stranger to her and how much it cost her to remain in touch with it". She added that she had at the same time understood she must "appear

3 Sister Teresia de Spiritu Sancto, *Edith Stein*, p. 114.

quite strange to those who lead active lives in the world".

Everything around Edith seemed to direct her to her truest vocation, beyond the intellectual life, beyond solitary prayer, beyond even the liturgical prayer of the corporate Church, leading her to the vocation which she hinted at in the final months of 1932, just before her entry into the Carmel: "There is a vocation which consists in suffering with Christ and thus in His redemptive work. If we are united to the Lord, we are members of His Mystical Body; Christ continues to live and suffer in His members, and suffering endured in union with Him becomes His, made efficacious and united in His great redemptive work. The essence of the religious life, especially the Carmelite life, is to intercede for sinners and cooperate in the redemption of the world by *voluntary and joyous* suffering."

When she left the Cologne Carmel, to take refuge in a Dutch Carmel, Edith wrote her "Memoirs." She gave them to her prioress as a "Christmas gift," in which she recounted some of the external circumstances of her vocation. In it, she recalled particularly one evening in the Lent of 1933, when, returning later from a meeting of Catholic intellectuals, she made her way, after the closing of the gates, into the College where she lived. A teacher there, recognizing her, invited Edith to spend the night at his apartment and, while his wife prepared a room for her, he told her what the American newspapers were publishing about the atrocities committed against the Jews in Germany. "Suddenly, it became clear to me that the hand of God lay heavily upon His people and that the destiny of His people was my own." On Thursday of Holy Week, Edith set out—as she had for the past five years—to the Benedictine Abbey of Beuron where she spent Holy Week and Easter. She planned to go to Rome to request the Holy Father to write an encyclical on the Jewish question, and she wanted to find out what the Abbot, Dom Walzer, then in Japan, thought of her idea before she went through with it. At this time, Edith was an Oblate of St. Benedict at Beuron Abbey. On her way, she stopped at Cologne and prayed in the Chapel of the Carmel: "I spoke interiorly to our Lord, telling Him that I *knew* it was His Cross weighing down upon our people. Most Jews did not recognize the Saviour, but was it not the lot of those who did know Him to bear His Cross? That is what I want to do. I asked Him only to show me how. And when the ceremony (Vigil of the First Friday of the month) in the chapel finished, I became certain that He had answered my prayer. I did not know then what His Cross would be for me."

The following day, Edith went to Beuron; the

Father Abbot advised her not to go to Rome, because, returning home, he had seen the conditions at Rome. When she arrived back at Münster, Edith learned that the officials had demanded that "Doctor Stein" quit teaching. Now nothing prevented her entry into the Carmel, since she could no longer carry any influence in the world, and the reason for holding back in the world was at last gone. "For almost twelve years, Carmel has been my one goal, from the first day back in 1921 when the *Life* of St. Teresa fell into my hands and brought my long search for the true faith to an end. When, on New Year's Day, 1922, I was baptized, I thought it but one more preparation for my entering the Order of Carmelite Nuns . . . ." But she did not enter the religious life at the express request of her spiritual advisors, and because of the grief she would necessarily bring to her mother. "Waiting had become very difficult for me. I had become a stranger in the world. . . ."

On April 30—Good Shepherd Sunday—after the Benediction of the Blessed Sacrament, she "received, inwardly, the Good Shepherd's consent", and that evening she wrote of her resolution to the Abbot of Beuron.

In May, Edith made contact with the Carmel of Cologne which was just preparing a new foundation in Breslau, the city of Edith's birth. Received by the Prioress, the Subprioress, and the Novice

Mistress, she told them of her long spiritual journey: "It always seemed that the Lord was keeping something for me in the Carmel which I could find only there."

On June 18 and 19, she returned to the Carmel of Cologne from Münster, underwent the scrutiny of the Chapter Nuns, and sang before them at their request: "It was harder for me than if I had delivered an address to a thousand people." On the following day, Edith received a telegram confirming her acceptance into the Carmel, and giving her permission to live at the Carmel for one month as a "guest", beginning July 15. "Six huge cases of books preceded me to Cologne ... The month passed outside the "enclosure" (of the Carmel) was one of great happiness. I observe the sisters' Rule, working during my free time; I often visited Mother Josepha (the Prioress) in the parlor and asked her any questions which happened to cross my mind. Her answers were always the ones I felt I would have made myself, and this agreement made me very happy."

On August 10, Edith went to Triers to receive the Abbot of Beuron's blessing, spending the Feast of the Assumption at the Abbey of Maria-Laach, and then went on to Breslau.

7 "IN THE DEEPEST SECURITY":
THE CARMEL

Edith told her family that "the sisters of the Cologne
Carmel had decided to accept her". They understood
her to mean that she would be going to a new
teaching post in October.... Edith's sister, Rosa,
waited for her at the Breslau station, and Edith
confided her plans to her. Rosa had put off joining
the Church in order to spare her mother any ad-
ditional pain.

Frau Stein had weathered practically everything,
but now she struggled vainly against the trials which
came to her from all sides. When the Jews were
officially barred from all public offices, who would
dare buy wood from the Jews, or even sell it to them?

Writing to a friend whom she especially asked
to pray for her mother, Edith concluded with: "In
the deepest security: *in tabernaculo Domini.*" The
suffering ahead of her was not hers alone, but belonged as well to her mother whom she loved more

than anything in the world, next to the Lord—and
Edith was to cause this grief because of the sum-
mons she could not but answer, and which was a
most necessary obligation rising from the immense
love that had taken hold of her entire life. And it
was the logical conclusion of her intellect entirely
dedicated to her Lord. There was no way out for
her. Driven by her love and fidelity to the truth,
Edith had to bring down a great sadness upon her
mother, whom she loved intensely, and add one
more grief to all her other sufferings at the very
time when her world was crumbling in about her,
and the foundations of the house she had so zealously
built had collapsed beneath her.

Edith's love for the persecuted Jews necessitated
that final step, for if she were to raise up to the Lord
a prayer sprung from a Jewish heart, and if she
were to really suffer the lot of the Jewish People,
she believed that she absolutely had to enter the
Carmel, even at the risk of breaking her mother's
heart. Abraham's sacrifice was realized, in Edith's
oblation, in blood and tears . . . .

"My mother," Edith wrote in her "Memoirs" to
the Prioress, "suffered intensely from the political
turn of events. She was continually upset from the
problems caused by "those evil men" (the Nazis and
their henchmen). And heaped on top of this agitation
was added a personal loss—her daughter Erna, now

a doctor, left home to live in another section of Breslau, and took her children with her: "Erna, her husband and children, were a joy and consolation for mother, and she bitterly resented their leaving."

Frau Stein "seemed to come to life again" with Edith's arrival: "When she came home from work in the evening, she enjoyed sitting down and knitting close by the desk where I worked, and she told me all that happened to her that day .... I got her to tell me all about the past .... My presence did a great amount for her. But I thought to myself: "If only you knew ...."

The dreaded day finally arrived when Frau Stein asked: "What are you going to do with the sisters at Cologne?" Edith answered, "To live with them", and there immediately folowed a "desperate attempt to dissuade her", after which Edith felt "a great wall had come between the two of us": "There was no peace from that day on." After Frau Stein had exhausted herself with these "angry outbursts", she succumbed to long "periods of silent despair".

"I had to take the step alone and wholly plunged into the darkness of faith", Edith wrote. No one around her understood, and her entry into the convent at the very moment when the Jews were suffering bitter persecution seemed a betrayal and desertion of her people. She knew, however, that she had decided upon this final step in order to give herself

completely to the Lord so that His grace might
shower down upon the Jewish world, so that He
might take pity on them, comfort them in their
suffering, and lead those who recognized Him into
the Church.

Edith set October 12, the Feast of the Taber-
nacles, called the Expiation, one of the greatest
Jewish feasts, her birthday as well, for her departure
to the Carmel. On the morning, before she left,
Edith went to the Synagogue with her mother, and
they walked home afterwards. Edith tried to ease
her mother's inner grief by stressing that these first
months at the Carmel were only a period of trial.
But Frau Stein knew her daughter, "If you have
decided to try out this life, it is because you intend
to persevere in it. . . ." Then she discussed the Rabbi's
sermon, and, as Edith acknowledged that one could
be devout in Judaism "if one has not learned anything beyond that," Frau Stein said, without calling
Christ by name, "I have nothing against him . . . . He
may well have been a good man. But why did he
have to make himself God?" At that instant, the dis-
cussion between mother and daughter touched the
very heart of the Jewish spiritual drama. Father
Danielou mentions in his book, *Scandaleuse Vérité*,
that a rabbi once told him, " 'You see, we Jews re-
proach Christ because he tried to change the Law.
God gave us the Law, and God alone can change what

He has given.'" "I said to him," continues Father Danielou, 'You could tell me nothing which would please me more... The Law was given by God, God alone can change what He has given; therefore, if Jesus thought He had the right to change the Law, it was because He thought He was God.'"

The agony of Edith's departure was softened by an act of great tenderness. Sitting down, the elderly woman—she was eighty-four years old—"buried her face in her hands" and wept. Edith went up behind her chair, and "pressed her poor, dear wizened head to my heart.... We remained so for a long while, until it was time to go to bed. I took her to her room, and for the first time in my life, helped her undress. Then I sat on her bed... until she told me to get some sleep. Neither of us slept that night."

Edith left the next morning, after one last loving embrace, and spent that night "in a profound peace" at the threshold of the house of the Lord, in the Carmel of Cologne.

In a testimony given on Edith, the Abbot of Beuron wrote that "she did not choose the little Carmel of Cologne in the hope of coming to live with a learned prioress and a group of highly educated nuns." At the Carmel "she was the only intellectual, and she soon became the least of the sisters there." She did not dream of asking permission to continue her philosophical work in the

7 *Edith Stein*

convent, nor did she authorize her friends to inter-
vene on her behalf to the Superiors of the Order
to grant her that permission: "Her sole desire was
to disappear, to lose herself in the Carmel." And
since she was inept in manual labor, she came to
rejoice in being one of the least of the servants,
and drew near to the very essence of humility. She
learned humility when she thought back on how
one religious only saw her as a sister who handled
a broom quite badly. She learned of humility when
she avowed to the Prioress that she had "a rough
time learning all the little rules". But all of this
she desired and had waited for so long.

The strict poverty of her cell symbolized the
silence of the exterior world for every word but the
word of God, and she had always desired this kind
of poverty. "There was no need at all to prepare
her for the life of renunciation," wrote the Abbot
of Beuron, "she entered the Carmel like a child
rushing into its mother's arms, joyful and singing,
without ever later regretting the choice she had
made."

Her new life was truly one of fulfillment, not of
renunciation. The serenity and peace she felt on the
train going to Carmel may shock us, surely, when
we consider that she had just left her mother in
bitter anguish. But, as she knew that in entering
into Catholic prayer, she was not betraying her

brethren in Israel, but instead was coming to serve them where they could be best served: near the God they did not know, so too, she knew that there she could best show how much she loved her mother by praying that Jesus might console her grief. Who, better than Jesus, knew the sufferings of a mother?

What looked like renunciation was really no such thing. Her breaking away from home was not what it looked like, and her seeming departure *from* life was in reality her entry *into* life. Once, Edith wrote to a religious who sought her advice, "I believe that the response we must make is *Fiat voluntas tua.* The Holy Rule and the Constitutions are for us the expression of the divine will. Our participation in the sacrifice of Christ consists in sacrificing our personal inclinations to them. Furthermore, charity demands that we adapt ourselves to the customs of the house and the tastes of the community. *If we do it to make glad the heart of Jesus, it will not be a constraint for us, but rather the exercise of freedom in what is more noble, a voluntary act of love towards our Bridegroom.*"

Edith continually radiated joy. She would tell the Prioress that she had never laughed so much as in the recreation periods at the Carmel. Hers was a spiritual joy rising out of her union with God, and it was also the childlike and carefree joy of a nature freed from extra burdens of its own making. But, in the midst of this new life there was a sharp thorn that drove her to intense prayers of supplication: every Friday, Edith wrote to her mother, but she never answered . . . .

Edith did find some difficulty in adapting to the community life. Her ineptitude in manual labor was a unique cross. She told Frau Conrad-Martius how difficult it was to get used to "all the little details of the religious life". But even these difficulties became a part of her joy, they were the small change of the immense treasure that she offered the Lord and which He redeemed in joy. The essence of this life which she had so long desired, hoped for and awaited, alone counted—the total oblation of herself to Him whom she loved, a lasting presence with Him, total absorption in Him, and therefore, always greater nearness to Him. How could Edith help but be joyful, and when news came to her from the outside, how could she not but offer these heartaches as a pledge of her love for her Lover?

On Sunday, April 15, 1934, Edith received the Carmelite habit: hempen sandals, fifteen decade rosary, the long brown robe. But first, before she could wear these, she donned a white satin wedding dress. April 15, Good Shepherd Sunday, was the anniversary of the day she had asked God to let her enter the Carmel. A few days later, Hitler set up the Popular Tribunal in Berlin, and on the first of May, he organized the Ministry of Science, Education and Popular Culture which permitted the pretentious nonsense of Rosenberg to become the philosophy of a whole people, and through these actions the Nazis could persecute the Jews and Catholics all the more. But Edith was completely absorbed in her interior joy . . . .

. . . Clothed in her wedding dress, Edith walked out of the cloister to greet her old friends and all who could come to see her: the Abbot of Beuron, who celebrated the High Mass, the Father Provincial of the Carmelite Order, her godmother Conrad-Martius, and a group of friends and students: Doctor Stein would henceforth become only Sister Benedicta. She chose this name to signify her gratitude and high esteem for the great renovator of Western monasticism.

At the sound of the bells, Edith was led up to the altar where white flowers greeted her from all sides—gifts of her former pupils, the Catholic Women's Associations, and her university friends:

"What do you seek?"

"The mercy of God, the poverty of the Order and the company of the sisters."

"Are you resolved to persevere until death?"

"Thus do I hope and desire, relying on the mercy of God and the prayer of the sisters."

The sisters opened the cloister: Edith entered,

carrying a lighted candle in her hand. Before her, the Carmelites, holding candles, in black and white habits, formed the community Edith was about to enter and become one of: the community of continual prayer, the ardent fire of the love which will never cease being expressed ... Edith kissed the Crucifix they held out to her ... The Prioress leading her by the hand, Edith now vested in the brown robe, returned from the grille and received the blessed scapular and cincture which she could never refer to as "her own": "Receive the sweet yoke of Christ and His burden which is light .... When you will become old, another will gird you ...."

Arms outstretched in the shape of a cross, Edith prostrated herself on the chapel floor. She was no more than a tiny white spot crowned with roses. The *Veni Creator* was intoned:

> Best of Comforters,
> Delightful and refreshing guest of the soul,
> Rest in toil, refreshment in the heat of day,
> solace in grief ...
> ... O most Blessed Light,
> Fill the hearts of your faithful ...
> ... Grant to those who trust in you
> The sevenfold gift of grace ....

Edith gave the kiss of peace to her new sisters:

Behold how good and pleasant it is
to dwell together in harmony...
...It is as the dew of Hermon which comes
down
from the mountains of Sion.... (Psalm 132)

Sister Benedicta now began to follow in the footsteps of Teresa; the oblation was offered, never to be taken back.

Yes, she had made the total gift of herself. The Father Provincial of the Carmelites knew how much was concealed in this *total* gift. And scarcely had Sister Benedicta entered the cloister than he asked her to take up intellectual work once again. In the Carmel, Edith was to write her most beautiful works: *The Mystery of Christmas, Eternal and Infinite Being, The Science of the Cross, Hymns to the Church.*

Edith put herself into "the hands of the Infant," the hands which "take and give at the same time": the hands "take the wisdom of the wise, who become as guileless as infants", for "before the Infant in the manger, their minds are layed bare". Does she not speak of her own experience in these words? "In the kindergarten of the spiritual life, when we begin to walk and let ourselves be led by God, we feel His presence very strongly. His hand holds us..." But the "dark night" comes "which steals over the soul when the divine light no longer shines ... God is always there, but He is hidden and He keeps silent". Why? "These are the Mysteries of God which we touch upon, and they cannot easily be understood." But "God became man to let us share in His divine life: that is the beginning and the final goal." To have this "share", this participation, "every man must suffer and die", he must "participate fully" and consent to the darkness of the dark night, because this "torment" is permitted by God "to compensate for the sins of another ...." "That is why we must say: May your will be done, especially in this dark night of the soul ...." Because our suffering, even the suffering of the "dark night" is joined to the suffering of Jesus made flesh, it is also joined in the Redemption. Christmas Eve recalls to our minds the beginning of this ascent which we must make.

We have seen the central light which Edith found for her life and which drew her to the Carmel; we have seen it spring first from her research and philosophical meditations. It was because, in pursuing Husserl's ideas further than he himself did, she sought to find out the one thing consistent in the existence of the universe, that she went beyond the universe of things and entered into that of Creation which gave it its existence and its meaning. The light she discovered brightened not only her life, but resolved her philosophical problems as well. Because she found the light of existence, she came to see in her philosophical work that the mind aided the soul in finding itself, and now the soul enlightened the mind, her intellect reached out to love, and love guided her intellect from then on.

Edith Stein read Heidegger's *Being and Time*. She knew the author and was interested in this new thinking. Formed by Husserl and her contact with Heidegger, she was well versed in the thought which made up the existentialistic current. This explains the one ground for complaint we have—her confusion between philosophy, which begins with the facts of experience and reason, and theology, which, while certainly making use of reason, uses it to better understand what we learn through Revelation. The characteristic mark of phenomenology and existentialism is the rejection of such distinctions in order to concentrate on the flux of being to glean its profoundest significance. Edith continued on this road, continually clarifying her philosophical research, guided by the light of Revelation which gives the ultimate meanings behind the realities of the world that philosophy examines: the individual, nature, and thought.

If we are to take *Eternal and Finite Being*[1] for what it is, that is, a book which thoroughly confuses

1 *Endliches und Ewiges Sein,* (Freiburg–Louvain, 1950).

theology and philosophy, at least let us be able to distinguish what was and what remains the touchstone for Edith's conversion. Conversion here is understood in its literal meaning: *a turning towards,* a turning of her mind to what must satisfy it. For Edith Stein, the *ego* was seen as an undeniable reality. The ego is certain of being in existence, certain about existing *in time,* for it sees itself as a "now" between a "nevermore" and a "not yet".

Thus, by experiencing the *being* we are, we come to know of an existence which is to come (our future). We *are* and yet we are not *all* that we are (the completed, but subsistent, past, the future which draws us and already forms us by its very summoning). From this experience—existentialism finally concludes that, if we are not what we are, it is because we are not—Edith Stein, on the contrary, concluded to what she called a Being which is simple, a pure Being, with no admixture of non-being, and therefore permanent, eternal: God.

That was the *philosophical* path of Edith Stein: she concluded her first philosophical meditation and polished it off in a really *Thomistic* style. But on the way, she did not neglect all the wealth of her existentialistic experience. She did not forget the analytic depth of Heidegger's dereliction: "This term expresses above all that man is found to exist without knowing how he came to be ... But the question of his origin is not done away with. However much one may try to ignore such a question ... it will irresistibly arise from the singularity of the human being which demands a self-sufficient Being to be the cause of everything and to be the cause of himself; which requires Him who moves what is moved."

She followed Heidegger—and anteceded more than one French existentialist—in the analysis of anxiety. But she considered also that the human being encounters joy. Heidegger said that each of us is as though "thrown into existence", and she forced this argument into a corner. Yes, we perceive ourselves as ineluctably participating in existence. But, just because anxiety and the possibility of being reduced to total or partial nothingness hovers over us, we perceive at the same time the existence of what made us to be and sustains us in existence.[2] There is something more existent than ourselves, possessing in Himself all the being He gives us, and gives meaning to the anxiety we feel if we imagine that it is possible for us to cease existing.

Having arrived to this contemplation of the Being, Edith was no longer in the realm of philosophy. Her spiritual life enters the picture here, and, perceiving this divine Being as a Trinity, it was still

2 Let us keep in mind that we present here only the barest outline of a highly intricate thought.

the spiritual life speaking to her. Let us not be disappointed, if in one place or another—the problem of Evil, for example—Edith did not follow the traditional routes. It was an entirely different matter—the encounter of a soul with the divine Eternity.

EDITH STEIN

8 THE SCIENCE OF THE CROSS: THE OFFERTORY. PERSECUTION, EXILE AND DEATH

Sister Teresa Benedicta of the Cross made her temporary vows on Easter Sunday, April 21, 1935. She was fully at home in her new life, and her heart experienced a blissful serenity. Edith slipped easily into the life of adoration and prayer she had so long desired, and found her fulfillment in this life. Everyone who saw her as a Carmelite speaks of the peace and joy radiating from her. Gertrude von Le Fort,[1] who knew Edith while she lived in the world, and later in the convent, describes her "radiant, almost transfigured countenance". A university friend used the same words in describing Edith: "Her happiness overwhelmed me." When asked whether she had become accustomed to the solitude, she answered, "I

1 Author of *The Eternal Woman,* and *The Song at the Scaffold,* from which Bernanos was inspired to write his *Dialogues des Carmelites,* and many other fine books.

was more alone throughout most of my years in the world than I have ever been here", and when a lady admired her saintliness in the religious life, Edith replied, "We gladly share the peace of the convent with you, but you must never attribute to mere human beings what continues to be a pure gift of God."[2] Dom Feuling saw her while she was in the cloister and judged her as "matured" both in her humanity and in her faith, "wholly spiritualized ... she transcended the world", and "attained that barely perceptible degree of experimental knowledge which St. Thomas attributes to the gifts of the Holy Spirit." "A soul offered up, wholly given to God. If the great Teresa of Avila's primary purpose is to lead her daughters to the mystical life and union with God by means of contemplation, I dare say that Sister Benedicta walked firmly up this road ...."[3]

In the meanwhile, beyond the convent walls, Germany degenerated into that seething world of hatred and violence which Edith had foreseen and feared. She was not afraid for her own safety—the total oblation of herself could only be achieved by the sacrifice of her life—but for her loved ones, her mother, brothers, sisters, all "her people". A friend

2 Sister Teresia de Spiritu Sancto, *Edith Stein*, cf. p. 181.
3 Ibid., cf. Part II, Chapter III.

who described her joy in the religious life, told her how happy she was to see her safely behind the grille of the Carmel: "Don't believe it," Edith retorted, "they will come after me even here. And in any event, I don't count on being spared."

In 1935, the year Edith took her temporary vows, Hitler legalized the Jewish persecutions. On September 15, at Nuremberg, Hitler spoke about the Jewish question, while promulgating the "law for the protection of German blood and honor", and the law was rigorously upheld that following December. Frau Stein, now in her eighty-eighth year, and her children were hunted outcasts with no rights or privileges whatsoever.

To see how well Edith accepted all these trials, we have but to flip through the pages of her *The Science of the Cross*,[4] which she wrote while at the Carmel. This book remained unpublished until 1950. Edith first of all described the degrees of grace introduced by St. John of the Cross—whose work she followed—up to the penetration of the Divine Mystery. But it is fully appreciated only through the dark night of the soul. She depicted this dark night, not symbolically, but as a spiritual reality into which

4 *Kreuzwissenschaft*, (Louvain-Freiburg, 1950). We readily see the six years of crucifixion reflected in the spiritual experience which united Edith to her master in spirituality.

the creature ascending towards God is plunged: "The
night is invisible and shapeless. And yet we perceive it ... closer to us than anything else. It has
become an intimate part of us." The light makes
things appear as they truly are, while the night
enshrouds them, "threatening to swallow us up as
well". What is in darkness is "invisible and form-
less ... like a shadow or threatening spectre."

Edith inversely depicted the obsession and perception of the Being who guided her to the Church
and its traditional philosophy. In the light of these
pages, one comes to understand how Edith the
philosopher approached and finally entered the
Church of Christ which alone answered her problems about complete and full existence. They illus-
trate how she confused her deductive philosophical
work and her theology which meditates upon the
experiences of the "other" given by Revelation.

Our existence, then, is "inwardly, not outwardly,
threatened by dangers lurking in this dark night".
In Sartre's existential "annihilation" of man, the
"dark night" of the mystics, Edith saw the only
solution, and knew its dramatic intensity. In the
immediately apparent emptiness that exists in the
world and in our hearts, certainly rational experience
begins to bear witness to the truth of an existence
acting on the world and revealing itself in relationships among men. Existential "nothingness" may

show up in the very heart of existence as the experience of the vanity and love of things. The night "depriving us of our senses, trammels our activity, paralyzes our faculties". This is a concise image of the night of the mind and soul, but it is much more than just an image, for this is an experience actually undergone by souls.

The "night" of the mystics is a language—God's language speaking and drawing souls ever nearer to His Being. The mystical night, seen as the *absence of God,* speaks of God and announces Him. "There is a soft nocturnal glow in a mind that is freed ... calmed and meditative before plunging into reality . . . ." The soul must consent to it and understand it as a test, a token of love awaiting love, if this night is to be at all beneficial to the soul. A "night" forcing the soul to withdraw into itself by refusing love is despair. And this is the path taken by more than one "existentialist", even before mystical experience. "If we agree to believe through faith,[5] and if we entirely accept Christ ... He will guide us by His Passion and Cross" to the glory of the Resurrection . . . . After the dark night has passed, the "Living Fire of Love" will "illumine the secret re-

5 We shall not go into the discussions raised over Edith Stein's definition of faith. Hilda C. Graef is evidently correct in preferring the definition of the *Epistle to the Hebrews* to that of Edith. Cf. *The Scholar and the Cross.*

lationships between God and the soul". "In this way, the spiritual marriage between the soul and God, for which God created it in the first place, will be achieved and consummated on the Cross and sealed with it for all eternity."

We cannot say, only the Church dares, precisely what Edith Stein's spiritual experience was. The light shed by some of her many letters of spiritual direction written at the Carmel, reveal the experience of a soul which found certitude in the joy of its love.

To one Dominican religious who asked whether the mystical graces are reserved to special people, Edith replied that "the decisive factor is conformity to the Divine Will. John of the Cross and Teresa of Avila saw this to be essential. The surest way for us is to empty ourselves of everything so that we can then be attentive to divine grace." This well-defines Edith's own life. And, from the inaccessible interior refuge which is anything but an escape, she looked the world squarely in the face and thought of the "priests and religious confined in prison" for whom "everything is grace" because they possess "God and the Trinity completely" within them.

We know how Edith came to the immense interior peace which nothing could shake, not even the trials or dangers pressing upon her. We know how because she depicted it in *The Prayer of the Church,* certainly one of her finest works.

Prayer dwelt within her from the very beginning of her spiritual journey before her Baptism. She recognized the two essential ideas of prayer. The first is that "The work of Redemption is consummated in secret and in silence. The living prayers which help form the Kingdom of God, the instruments He chooses to work with, are cut and honed in silent dialogue between souls and Him." The second is that personal prayer, individual prayer and the prayer of the Church are one reality, one flowing stream: "The torrent of mystical graces running through the ages forms the principle and deepest part of the stream of the Church's prayer, and there are no diverted branches to this stream."[6]

In her long encounters with the Lord, Edith knew and desired even before entering the Carmel. She understood that the mystical life and prayer were not separate, but that each supported and naturally engendered the other. She wanted and loved the Divine Office sung in common, and she practiced it during her long contact with the Benedictine religious before entering the Carmelite Order. This experience helped her to better understand how there can be but one prayer, and not individual or group prayer: "The Divine Office passes the

6 *The Prayer of the Church.* This translation is made from the French text of the *Editions de l'Orante*—Tr.

News from one generation to the other.[7] A great many voices fade into one another and are lost as though swept away in the rushing torrent of the mystical stream whose booming sound rises up in a canticle of praise to the Holy Trinity, God, Creator, Redeemer and Lifegiver. It is wrong to separate or set in opposition to each other subjective personal prayer and objective social, liturgical prayer. Every true prayer is the prayer of the Church, every prayer operates in it, and the whole Church prays in every prayer, for the Holy Spirit dwells in it."[8]

Edith wanted to express all she saw in prayer and professed with every ounce of her being by putting the conclusion of the Canon of the Mass into a chapter heading on *The Prayer of the Church*: "By Him and with Him and in Him are given to You, God the Father Almighty, in the unity of the Holy Spirit all honor and glory for ever and ever."

Our reality and prayer, the Church's reality and prayer are not two distinct realities, two paths to God. We only have existence through participation in Him Who Is. We pray only when our prayer joins in with the great praise of all souls throughout the earth which alone validly expresses Him in the

7 Edith did not mean this to be interpreted as the singular function of the community Office which expresses the Church.

8 *La Prière de l'Eglise* (Paderborn, 1936).

sacrifice of the One in whom all prayer finds its source and meaning. Our prayer exists only because it is rooted in total Offering and is one with the Church.

"Christ is the center of the universe and offers Himself for it and became man to renew it inwardly and bring it to perfection. He calls upon the whole of the created universe to give thanks to the Creator in union with Him."[9] Edith guessed at the "Eucharistic meaning of prayer" from the outset of her spiritual journey. She expressed it by citing the Psalmist: "I love the beauty of Your house, the dwelling place of Your glory", which led her to the foot of the altar, long before entering into the joy of the Carmel. She outwardly manifested this truth in her hieratic attitude before the altar. Some people considered her cold and distant because of this. One religious said that "she couldn't understand how one might stand so long before the Eucharist without growing weary". This was Edith's personification of her total union in Christ.

Pray to be united, be united to pray—this is a double progression. He who prays is offered and asks to be joined with Christ's merits. He asks that his offering be made acceptable and requests the grace necessary for his prayers to be received and

9 *La Prière de l'Eglise.*

united to the merits of the Holy Passion. *Opus Dei,* the liturgical prayer *acts* so that God might wait for us. It is also the *work* of God within us, transforming our being into what He waits for.

True, Jesus prayed alone, but He prayed with the people also, and expects us to pray together, until at length "all may be one". "Where would soldiers be without their captain?" asked St. Teresa. Personal prayer is valid because it is united to the prayer of the Church and the communal Eucharist which alone prefigures the Eternal Unity.

At the apex of the spiritual life, Edith never forgot the world. Neither did her great patron saint. Edith and Teresa both saw the world is best served in the heart of prayer: "The Lord alone knows how much the prayer of St. Teresa and her daughters contributed to safeguard Spain from heresy. God alone knows what power they wielded in the bitter religious wars in France, the Low Countries and the Germanic Empire."

Because Edith saw this fact, she always preserved her deep interior peace and imperturbable, almost rash, calmness, while her loved ones sank beneath the oppressive Nazi tyranny.

During those frightful days, she wrote *The Science of the Cross,* and Providence prepared her for worse things to come.

After long sufferings, Frau Stein died on September 15, 1936. They tried to tell Edith her mother died a Christian, but she refused to believe them because she knew in her heart that her mother had died praying in the Jewish Faith. Rosa, waiting until after her mother's death, received the sacrament of Baptism and then rejoined her sister, who, by a fortunate accident, was in the hospital. There they could visit freely. It happened that one night the Prioress heard a delicate cough along the darkened staircase of the convent, and went to investigate. There she found Edith who had fallen in the darkness and broken her hand and foot. Edith coughed because the Rule forbade any infraction of the grand silence.

Rosa was baptized on Christmas Eve.

The Carmel of Cologne began its preparations for celebrating the three hundredth year of its founding. Edith did her share of the work, and at the same time kept up a vast correspondence giving spiritual direction to other religious, priests included.

On April 21, 1938, Edith took her final vows, while all about her the world seethed at the brink of war, vividly reminding her why she was offering herself to God. Six days after her solemn profession Husserl died. Being non-Aryan, he lost his professorship at Freiburg and took refuge in the convent of St. Lioba where Edith had often gone to pray, and one of her own students entered after being converted. Husserl had something akin to a vision on Good Friday, seeing "light and darkness; a great darkness and, once again, the reappearance of a light".

Ten days before her profession, April 10, 1938, Germany's national elections brought the Nazi Party 99 per cent control over the Reichstag. A month earlier, Hitler entered Vienna.

The religious were obliged to vote in this election, and Edith urged them to vote against Hitler. On the morning of the balloting, several government officials brought a ballot-box into the convent parlor, so they would have no trouble in finding out just *how* they voted. The Prioress objected in vain, and they had to cast their ballots immediately. The officials noticed that "Doctor Edith Stein" did not vote, and the sisters told them that she was a "non-Aryan", whereupon one of them noted the "admission" in writing.[10]

Edith's brother, her sister Erna and children left Germany before the persecutions got under way. In September of 1938, Hitler began his campaign to unite the Sudetenlands to Germany, and occupied the territory in October. On November 9, the pogroms broke out throughout the length and breadth of

10 At the time of the voting, the Prioress thought it advisable for Edith to vote without divulging her origins.

Germany. The Cologne Synagogue was burned. Edith wrote, "The shadow of the Cross has fallen over my people." It also fell over her.

Edith agreed to take refuge in Holland in the Echt Carmel which took in the Carmelite refugees from Cologne during the *Kulturkampf*.[11] She crossed the frontier on the foggy night of December 31, and the sisters at Echt welcomed her. Rosa would soon join her there.

On Passion Sunday (1939), Edith wrote her Superior for permission to "offer herself to the Sacred Heart of Jesus as a sacrifice of atonement for the peace of the world". She added that "If the reign of Antichrist could be shortened without another world war ... I should offer myself today, for it is the twelfth hour. I know I am nothing, but Jesus desires it, and He will doubtlessly request it of many other souls."

In the midst of so many perils, the sisters of Echt admired her "gaiety". In a letter of November, 1940, to her friend Conrad-Martius, she remembered to thank her for "the many fine mirabelle plums" the convent owed to the excellent horticultural advice of Hans Conrad-Martius .... In the summer of 1940, Rosa in her turn crossed the frontier and

11 Bismarck's long struggle against Catholicism.

joined her sister .... They were never again to be separated.

Now began the silence of prayer where death was more real than the turmoil of life. It is quite evident that during her final months on earth, Edith passed into the world in which St. John of the Cross had been utterly absorbed.[12] She wrote: "By *pure love* our Father St. John understood the love of God for God Himself, by a heart free from all attachment to created things, free from self and others, free even from all the consolation which God gives a soul, that is, *a heart which only desires the accomplishment of the will of God and is guided by Him without the least resistance* .... Must we try to attain this state of pure love? Most surely, for it is the end to which we have been created. It will be our eternal life, and we must come as close to it on earth as possible. Jesus is made man to be our life. What can we do? Struggle with all our might to become detached from all things ... Empty our minds of all natural curiosity by fixing on God the simple regard of our faith ...." (Letter of March 13, 1940.) Edith surrendered wholly to such a detachment.

Edith and Rosa visited in the parlor on Sundays. She brought Edith news of the ominous turmoil

12 She completed *The Science of the Cross.*

wracking the world. She told Edith of the persecutions of Jews and Catholics. The nuns at Echt
learned of the great upheaval in many ways, not
the least of which was the engine throb of glutted
bombers coming and going over the Carmel to
destroy German and British cities.

Edith kept busy with writing the life of Sister
Aimée de Jesus. She launched into the mystique of
Pseudo-Dionysius and taught Latin to the novices:
"They are excellent students, and give me much
joy. What a tremendous grace it is to have so many
young people in our little family of sisters who are
all somewhat up in years." The "older" convent
family sometimes looked disconcertingly upon Edith
who was dispensed from all the community's manual
labor so that she could devote all her free time to
study. They were upset too because she brought an
uneasiness into the house when they heard Rosa tell
them of the war and persecutions. They were afraid
Edith would attract unfavorable attention to the
convent. In the midst of all this, Edith abandoned
herself to the "detachment" of St. John of the Cross.

The Carmelite who asked Christ to fill her with
"emptiness" was not at all blind or deaf to what was
going on around her. She knew her desire to be
offered for the Jewish people was soon to be fulfilled.
It was a grace that her offering had been accepted,
but if she really *knew* of this acceptance, it would

have been a grave cause for spiritual pride. Yet, she continually offered herself for "others", the "others" with whom she lived, because the responsibility of sin is common, and still more, perhaps, because she wanted to help save "her Jewish people". "I think mostly of the responsibility we all share in others' guilt", she wrote commenting on Psalm XVIII.[13]

"The others": the Jews who crucified Jesus, the Nazis who persecuted the Jews ... and all "others" indifferent to the persecution, indifferent to love .... Beyond this, enduring it, she hoped and longed for the "emptiness" of fulfillment ....

Edith felt the sun over her brief existence begin to set. Everything had been taken away from her— or rather, she had given all: her family, her two "nations", Germany and the Jewish People, her university life, and her spiritual family at Cologne. Alone in a new convent in a foreign land, with only Rosa—her only tie to her former life—to bring news of hatred and persecution in the world beyond the cloister. She still clung to the hope-filled "emptiness" of her Father, John of the Cross: "The history of monastic souls is a marvelous one. They are deeply hidden away in the divine Heart. And *what we so often believe we understand is but a pale reflection of what remains the mystery of God until the day*

13 Verses 13 and 14.

*when all will be revealed to us. MY GREATEST
JOY IS THE HOPE IN THE LIGHT TO COME."*

While discussing Pseudo-Dionysius, she wrote,
"The prophet has no need to see God with his eyes
or his imagination, and in spite of all evidence to
the contrary, he has the interior certitude that God
speaks to him." She employed the impersonal "one"
where her own personal experience seemed to be
speaking: "This certitude is perhaps founded on
the feeling that God is present. One feels touched
by Him who is in the most intimate center of our
being. This is, strictly speaking, what one calls *the
experience of God,* essential to every mystical experience where one encounters God as one creature
meets another...."

For some time, the Carmel at Echt had planned
to get Edith into a neutral country. The Swiss Carmel
of Paquier agreed to accept her. But Edith could
not leave without Rosa. Thinking back on it now,
we might think that they began negotiating for a
Swiss passport too late. Regardless, Edith and Rosa
were called to Maestricht by the Gestapo. Upon
entering the office, Edith saluted, not with the usual
"Heil Hitler", but the "Praised be Jesus Christ" of
the convent. They broke the law by not wearing
the yellow "Star of David" on their outer garments.
They were summoned again in May to the inquisitors
of the Jewish Commission in Amsterdam. One

officer told Edith about the bombing of Cologne and the destruction of Holy Mary of the Peace where Edith paused to pray before crossing the frontier.

Several priests advised her to escape "illegally", but she refused to do this because she would not have her sisters suffer the consequences of her escape.

On July 11, 1941, the Dutch Catholic Hierarchy solemnly protested against the Jewish persecutions. On July 28, Edith learned that her brother Paul was taken with his family and sister Freida to a concentration camp (by coincidence to Theresienstadt). Edith doubted she could secure a passport for Switzerland, and wrote: "I shall accept everything God wills" and "For several months I have worn over my heart a verse from the Gospel of St. Matthew: 'When they persecute you in the city, flee to another. I tell you truly that you will not have gone to all the cities of Israel when the Son of Man comes.'"

On August 2, in reprisal to the letter promulgated by the Dutch Hierarchy speaking out against the persecution and formally stating that the Christians of Jewish origin could not be deported (the Germans forbade publishing this measure), all Catholic "non-Aryans" were arrested in Holland. At five o'clock in the evening, while the sisters were in choir, the Prioress was called to the parlor by two German officers. Believing they came to give her the passports for Switzerland, she signaled for Edith. One of the Germans ordered Edith to leave "in five minutes". Edith replied, "I cannot. The Rule of cloister forbids it."

"Get this out of the way (the grille) and come out," the officer demanded.

Edith replied calmly, "I must not leave."

The officer called the Prioress, and Edith returned to choir to kneel before the Blessed Sacrament, while the Prioress argued with the officer:

"Sister Stein must leave the convent in five minutes . . ."

"But, the Stein sisters are waiting for their passports . . ."

"That will be taken care of later. Give her a blanket and three days' rations."

Rosa knelt before the cloister for the Prioress' final blessing. Edith came down from her cell surrounded by the sisters, and then they left together . . . They heard her tell the German that she was still waiting for a passport . . . "The street was crowded with people protesting this outrage . . . . At the streetcorner the Gestapo police van waited for them . . . ."

That evening, the newspapers carried an article by the German General-Kommissar: Because the Dutch Hierarchy refused to "respect the confidential nature of these negotiations", the German authorities

must "consider Jewish Catholics as their worst ene-
mies" and "see to it that they are deported with all
dispatch to the East" (August 3, 1942).

Two police vans, one carrying thirteen, the other
seventeen, prisoners, the Stein sisters included, arrived at Amersfoort at three in the morning, and
were promptly beaten with cudgels and cast into a
hut without being fed.

On August 5, a telegram came from the muni-
cipality of Westerbork, in Northern Holland, asking
for clothing, blankets and medicine supplies for
the Stein sisters. Included in the packet the sisters
at Echt sent off was a holy card on which Edith had
written her wish to sacrifice her life for the conversion
of the Jews.

At the prison camp, Edith met her friend Ruth
Kantorowicz, taken from the Ursuline nuns in Venloo. The young men sent with clothing and other
necessary items from the convent saw her. While
telling them what had happened since leaving the
convent, "she was calm and serene": "Her eyes shone
with the mysterious radiance of saintliness. Quietly
and soberly, she described all that happened to
those around her, but never touched on her own
troubles. She was especially desirous the sisters be
told that she still wore her religious habit, and that
it was her intention and the intention of all the
religious (there were about ten of them) to keep on

wearing them until the end. She described the joy of the other prisoners in learning that priests and sisters were numbered among them. They became the one hope and support to these poor people who were expecting the very worst at any time. She was glad to give her fellow-prisoners any consolation by word and prayer. Her deep faith created an atmosphere of grace and peace around her. Several times she insisted that we reassure the Reverend Mother and the sisters... She prayed almost all day long, except when she had to get her food. She never spoke one word of complaint...."[14]

The messenger sent from the convent of Venloo saw Edith and Ruth Kantorowicz. Edith told them, "Whatever happens, I am prepared. The Child Jesus is with us even here...."

Two survivors of the frightful odyssey brought back the account of what happened to her, and we fully reproduce it here. The first is from a Jewish business-man: "Sister Benedicta stood out from among those brought to the prison camp (Westerbork) on the fifth of August, because of her great calmness and recollection. The cries, distress and confused state of the new arrivals was indescribable. Sister Benedicta went among the women as an

14 Account written by the young men sent from the convent to the sisters.

angel of mercy, calming and helping them. Many of the mothers were on the verge of madness, succumbing to a black and brooding melancholia. They neglected their children and could only weep in dumb despair. Sister Benedicta took care of the little children, washing and combing them, and bringing them food and looked after their other basic needs."

Another eyewitness writes: "Her silence distinguishes Edith from the other religious. She seemed to me to be suffering immensely, but peacefully. I can't express it any better than by saying that she seemed to carry such suffering on her shoulders that even her smile languished. She rarely spoke and often cast inexpressibly sad glances at her sister Rosa ... She thought about the trials she had foreseen—not her trials, but those of the others." The looks she gave Rosa show us how she suffered for others, but she continually prayed and filled her soul with peace.

On August 6, she managed to get a few lines through to the Prioress, telling of the departure of the first convoy for Silesia or Czechoslovakia. She asked for wool stockings, blankets, woolen underclothing, a crucifix and rosary for Rosa. For herself she requested the next volume of the Breviary, and their identification cards. She added: "So far, prayer has been coming along *marvelously.*"

On August 7, one of Edith's former pupils, standing on the platform of the Schifferstadt railroad station, heard Edith call out from the train, "Greet the sisters of St. Magdalena for me. I am headed East."

Another message to the Prioress—undated—contained just a few lines: "Under the present circumstances, it is better I try nothing more.[15] In any event, I commit myself entirely into your Reverence's hands and whatever you decide to do. *I am quite content now. One can only learn the* Scientia Crucis *if one truly suffers under the weight of the Cross. I was entirely convinced of this from the very first and I have said with all my heart*: Ave Crux, Spes Unica."

The *Official Journal* of Holland, on February 16, 1950, published the following lines in a list of the victims of the deportation:

> No. 44074 — Edith — Teresa — Hedwige STEIN — born 12 October, 1891, in Breslau — Arrived from Echt — died 9 August, 1943 (typographical error; it should have read 1942, and the same for Rosa whose date the *Official Journal* gave as 4 May, 1950:)

15 Meaning to escape or get them safely to Switzerland. They both hoped for Switzerland until the last moment.

No. 44075 — Rosa — Maria — Agnes — Adelaide STEIN — born 13 December, 1883 at Lublinitz (Ger.) — Arrived from Echt — died 9 August, 1942.

We know nothing more about them except that they were killed at Auschwitz.[16]

The Carmelites of Cologne announced Sister Benedicta's death, and concluded with:

"We shall look for her here on earth no longer, for she has been called to God who accepted her sacrifice which will bear much fruit in the people for whom she prayed, suffered and died."

EDITH STEIN

9 THE MESSAGE OF EDITH STEIN

What is a conversion? The word itself means "a turning towards". The religious, the Catholic conversion, is a turning towards the Love which is the creative act of the entire universe, expressed at every moment in keeping the universe and all creatures in the state of being. Love made man to take upon Himself all the evil in humanity is the Sustainer of the universe. He has given Himself up freely to be crucified so that He could use absolute evil as an instrument to save the world.

Conversion to Catholicism is to understand the beginning and the end of every created being. It is to live one's whole life in trying to better understand this. It is the turning of one's whole being to the Light which illumines the mind, and to the All-Powerful who brought the world into existence.

No one was more thoroughly *converted* than Edith Stein.

If life is so profoundly meaningful, then no conversion is more significant for our age than hers.

Because her intellect caught sight of the total
necessity, Edith began to take her first shaky steps
on the road to the Faith. She took them out of
rational necessity. Edith was not led by sentiment
or her heart, and her motives were not properly
religious ones.

From the very beginning, Edith Stein probed
deeply into the mystery of the world and was not
satisfied with merely examining the surface appearances of things and the universe. She was a wholly
logical woman. She was one who from the outset—
like her whole epoch, but with more of an insight,
more complete exigency—rejected an "idealism"
with which the post-Cartesian mind only toyed with
superficial ideas of reality. Her mind had to examine
the whole complexity of existence, for if it did not,
she saw that it would only waste itself in useless
and dishonorable sport.

But, at this stage in her progression, Edith perceived, along with Max Scheler and others, that one
cannot enter into the very heart of things, one cannot enter into being, without *sympathy*, without
participation and communion. Here, she desired to
grasp the world by fully understanding it, she wanted
to enter into Existence *with* others, in the fellowship
of destinies which have not got their full existence,

which only come to fully know themselves as Beings if each projects on the other the "image" of a love that becomes knowledge because it is participation in a birth in Being.

And here, we must recognize that Edith Stein is in some way the answer to a shallow existentialism. It is true that, if we do not welcome them in existence with love, we reduce others to nothingness, we *annihilate* them, while reducing our own selves to nothingness. Then, it is only too true that "hell is others". There is no being without love. Love is as the interior light of the world which, if it disappears, reduced all that *could be* to the nothingness of darkness. But with an act of love, all comes into being.

Now God made this act of love by the perpetual rebirth which is creation, and by sharing His loving act with each member of creation. Golgotha bore witness to the perfection of His Creative Love. When Edith turned herself entirely towards the universal Being, she could not avoid encountering the Crucified's act of love—and she encountered Him . . . .

. . . She experienced it because she met some men and women who lived this love and, in living it, brought life.

She encountered it and *prolonged* it until she offered herself for "her people".

Some have rightly said that Edith Stein's life is more important than what she wrote. To be exact, whatever she wrote only has full meaning in the light of what she was.

In *turning towards* Christ, she turned herself towards the most traditional philosophy of the Church, Thomism. We can argue about how she sometimes used Thomistic thought. But the important thing is that she knew how to advance by the strength of her whole being, by the meaning of her entire life. She came to see that to understand the universe one had to come to see that it demanded the light of love, and the light of love gave the intellect much more in return.

Edith Stein is a marvelous example of the "Christian philosopher" over which great controversies have arisen during the last quarter century. "The love of God will always be more noble than his knowledge .... But submission, the proper act of love, will tend towards intellection. The act of being united, thoroughly, will be to know."[1] The little Jewess of Breslau constantly reached out for this rigorous knowledge, strengthened in her journey by the lesson of mandatory exactitude learned from the Synagogue.

Being and knowing are one and the same God. We struggle along the path of knowledge and love like poor, exhausted travellers, and the path is that

1 Rousselot, *The Intellectualism of St. Thomas.*

wonderful reconciliation of the faculties of being, something hard for us to perceive. And, failing to grasp at the same time the two ends of the chain, we rush headlong into the insane illusion of understanding without loving, and into the disheartening resignation of loving without understanding. We are tossed about from pride to despair, finding repose only in a despair proud in resignation.

Edith Stein saw that "I find myself constantly on the verge of annihilation and I must receive being at every instant." To this truth, Edith dedicated the certainty of her death offered and consented to. The most desperate of existentialisms says what Edith said. But she went on to say that it suffices for one ounce of love and *sacrificing* to secure access to the infinite kingdom of being which is not given in exchange, but freely offered.

The very *certitude* of Edith on the road to Auschwitz—"I am quite content now"—is the only response to the existential *anxiety*. No one can deny the infinite reality of this anxiety. It is in every one of us, lurking in the heart of a mystic, and in the soul of everything that *is*: our being is not *ours*, it is parcelled out one instant at a time. An expression of hatred or omission can throw us out of being and into nothingness.

But the world is there to teach us its lesson. The slow plodding of human reason up the ladder of creation tells us that *all things have meaning,* provided we look upon the world with love.

One day perhaps the Church will declare Edith Stein a saint. For us, she is already the patroness of the unity of knowledge and love. Edith told her despairing times that it was right to despair because it then separated knowledge from love, and this was the road of denial; but the other path is there. We have only to turn our gaze, like her . . . .

The Synagogue taught Edith the way to love by instilling in her the desire for exactitude. This book is the testimony of a love which came to know the beloved through respect for knowledge.

To edit, to print, to publish, to promote: that is the apostolic effort of Alba House, staffed by the Pauline Fathers and Brothers. Alba House is part of the Pauline mission — to use modern communications techniques as a means of preaching and teaching Christian principles.

Paulines reach thousands daily — by each book, pamphlet, production. It is their calling in the Church to staff editorial offices, publishing plants, film studios, etc., and to develop for Christ those fields of communications still comparatively un-tapped. The Vatican Council's decree on the media of social communication has been a source of renewed energy.

International in scope, the Pauline Fathers and Brothers are located in twenty-three countries, with headquarters in Rome. In the United States they are in New York City, Buffalo, Detroit, Boston and Youngstown.

Literature on the Society of St. Paul can be obtained by writing to: The Pauline Fathers and Brothers, Vocation Office, 2187 Victory Blvd., Staten Island, N.Y. 10314